# Across the Galactic Sea

Copyright © 2012 Wayne J. Lutz

1st Edition printed 2012: ISBN 978-1-927438-10-7

All rights reserved. No part of this publication may be reproduced, stored in a retrieval system, or transmitted, in any form or by any means, electronic, mechanical, photocopying, recording, or otherwise, without the written prior permission of the author. Reviewers are authorized to quote short passages within a book review, as permitted under the United States Copyright Act of 1976.

Note for Librarians: a catalog record for this book that includes Dewey Decimal Classification and U.S. Library of Congress numbers is available from the Library and Archives of Canada. The complete catalog record can be obtained from their online database at:
www.collectionscanada.ca/amicus/index-e.html

ISBN 978-1-927438-10-7
**Printed in the United States**

# Powell River Books
Powell River BC, Canada

Book sales online at:
www.powellriverbooks.com
phone: 604-483-1704
email: wlutz@mtsac.edu

10 9 8 7 6 5 4 3 2 1

# Across the Galactic Sea

*Wayne J. Lutz*

2012
*Powell River Books*

# Books by Wayne J. Lutz

### *Coastal British Columbia Stories*
*Up the Lake*
*Up the Main*
*Up the Winter Trail*
*Up the Strait*
*Up the Airway*
*Farther Up the Lake*
*Farther Up the Main*
*Farther Up the Strait*
*Cabin Number 5*
*Off the Grid*
*Up the Inlet*

### *Science Fiction Titles*
*Echo of a Distant Planet*
*Inbound to Earth*
*Anomaly at Fortune lake*
*When Galaxies Collide*
*Across the Galactic Sea*

**Cover Photos:**

Front Cover – Pleiades (Messier 45) open star cluster; image from Hubble Space Telescope

Back Cover – Albireo double star in Cynus; image from Hubble Space Telescope.

# Contents

1 – If I Only Had a Brain . . . . . . . . . . . 6
2 – When Senility Sets In . . . . . . . . . . 9
3 – Near-Galactic Voyage . . . . . . . . . . 11
4 – Donut Holes . . . . . . . . . . . . . . . 17
5 – Thomson Jump . . . . . . . . . . . . . 28
6 – Bedside Manner . . . . . . . . . . . . . 36
7 – Girlfriends . . . . . . . . . . . . . . . . 43
8 – To Sleep, Perchance to Dream . . . . . 47
9 – Bulls-Eye . . . . . . . . . . . . . . . . . 52
10 – Glitch . . . . . . . . . . . . . . . . . . 58
11 – Noodles . . . . . . . . . . . . . . . . . 66
12 – Nixon's Tapes . . . . . . . . . . . . . . 73
13 – Poseidon . . . . . . . . . . . . . . . . 79
14 – Houston, We Have a Problem . . . . . 89
15 – Bow Camera . . . . . . . . . . . . . . 99
16 – Blink Test . . . . . . . . . . . . . . . . 103
17 – Stun Guns . . . . . . . . . . . . . . . 110
18 – 1420 Megahertz . . . . . . . . . . . . 117
19 – Rendezvous . . . . . . . . . . . . . . . 127
20 – Beyond the Realm of Earth . . . . . . 139
21 – EVA . . . . . . . . . . . . . . . . . . . 146
22 – Hitchhikers . . . . . . . . . . . . . . . 155
23 – Garden . . . . . . . . . . . . . . . . . 168
24 – Home . . . . . . . . . . . . . . . . . . 175
About the Author . . . . . . . . . . . . . . 182

## Chapter 1

## If I Only Had a Brain

Cougar awoke with a mind she didn't recognize. She knew – or thought she knew – who she was, but this definitely wasn't her brain.

On long voyages like this, almost anything could happen. Need a new heart? – We can do that. Need a new brain? – We probably can do that, too. The most amazing part was that she remembered who she was, or at least who she used to be.

As she slowly regained consciousness after five Earth-years of cryogenic hibernation, her head hurt the worst, but the rest of her body followed suit. Awakening after such a long sleep could rival the worst hangover imaginable. For Cougar, this was a chilling and throbbing aftereffect that hurt all over, dominated by a headache that competed for her immediate attention. Plus, she needed to throw up.

She remembered the discussion about her brain. During the first year of the mission, just before the first scheduled cryogenic period, Doctor Mercedes had diagnosed the problem, and the results were disturbing, to say the very least. Her hallucinations and frontal lobe pain were physical in origin, requiring brain surgery to correct the problem, and the odds weren't good for such an extensive surgical procedure in outer space during Earth's first truly galactic mission. While speeding out of the solar system – just now reaching their maximum rated continuous velocity of 0.13 SOL (speed of light) – Cougar presented an unexpected complication to the flight plan.

Then again, unusual complexities were where manned spaceflight thrived. Houston, we have a problem. Our NavCom officer needs brain surgery, and we're just setting up for five years of cryogenic hibernation, to be followed almost immediately by a Thomson-Jump to a target 33 light-years farther down the line, and then another hibernation period at cruise for five more years, et cetera, et cetera. Complicated enough without berserk brains.

Since two-way communication with Earth already lagged by several months, the mission planners at home would have nothing to contribute to the decision. Captain Tina Brett's judgment call was to proceed with the surgery, although Doctor Mercedes would lose five years of his life in the process. The flight plan couldn't be significantly altered without the entire mission being scrapped, and that meant the hibernation period had to continue on schedule. Which led to Captain Brett's resolve regarding brain surgery for Cougar and a recovery separate from the frozen sleep of the rest of the crew. While everyone else slept, Don Mercedes would try to save the life of Cougar Jensen. Afterwards, he'd have to figure out how to fill five years of a hermitic existence in space, since putting yourself into cryogenic sleep was reserved for emergencies only, and this was little more than "medical routine." Spacecraft crews either entered the frozen state as a group in "automated hibernation," supervised by the ship's artificial intelligence, or one at a time while overseen by another crewmember. In effect, Doctor Mercedes drew the short straw dictated by a flight manual logic tree that was based on centuries of military discipline.

It wasn't a huge obstacle for Doctor Donald Mercedes, considering his personality. Cougar had never met a man who seemed so removed from society. To say he didn't have much bedside manner was an understatement. In fact, he had little manner at all. Then again, he was undoubtedly the most qualified physician for this space mission, temperament be damned. In the various considerations open to Captain Tina Brett, his minimal bedside demeanor had nothing to do with the flight manual's logic tree. But if anyone could survive for an extended period without direct human contact, Don Mercedes was the perfect candidate.

He would anesthetize Cougar for the operation after the rest of the crew settled into their scheduled sleep. The brain surgery could then proceed on whatever schedule Mercedes felt was best. He would arrange Cougar's cryogenic sleep commensurate with her recovery from the surgical procedure. When Cougar awoke with the rest of the crew, she would (hopefully) be fully recovered and ready to return to work as the ship's NavCom officer. Meanwhile, Doctor Mercedes would be free to spend his next five years as he desired – the ultimate unscheduled vacation that would steal a half-decade of his life. When the rest of the crew awoke, they would find the doctor five years older, while the balance of the ship's company remained as ageless as the moment they were frozen.

Just when all of these arrangements (complications) were complete, word was received from Earth concurring with the verdict Captain Brett was already in the process of implementing. This was merely a confirmation of what was going to happen anyway. Captain Tina Brett could now go to sleep knowing Earth's last somewhat-direct communication was a command she was obeying.

She would have slept well anyway.

## Chapter 2

### When Senility Sets In

Cougar Jensen went to sleep after her brain surgery, and awoke while still 34 years old, and just as feisty as ever. But right now, she needed to throw up.

"You look pretty good, Doctor Don," said Cougar, taking into account his expected aging, to say nothing of the toll of loneliness.

"Well, you look like shit," replied Donald Mercedes with a smirk. "But your brain is working. I hope you don't mind the touch of kleptomania I added for good measure."

"So that's why I feel like stealing your ugly stethoscope."

Cougar couldn't remember seeing any other doctor with an old-fashioned stethoscope draped around his neck. The ancient device had been replaced by digital cardiometers centuries ago, but Doctor Mercedes was seldom seen without his unstate-of-the-art instrument. Actually, Cougar had liked Don Mercedes since she first met him during training for the mission. Sure, he didn't have a normal personality, but she felt comfortable with him while others mocked all of his quirks. Besides, he'd saved her life, while sacrificing five years of his own existence.

"Headache?" he asked, as she sat on the edge of the bed in her blue hospital gown, bare pale legs dangling towards the floor.

"You bet. A whopper. But more to the point – I need to puke."

Right on cue, Doctor Mercedes held a small plastic tray in front of her, as if he'd been concealing it behind his back, waiting for her to ask. As soon as she saw it, she immediately arched forward and tried to vomit, but nothing came up. She dry-heaved again, and then spit in the tray, relieved to see it looked like the normal putrid phlegm expected after five years of sleep.

"Sorry, not very lady-like," she said, not sounding a bit apologetic.

"We'll need to get you some crackers before giving you anything for that headache. Shouldn't take pills on an empty stomach, you know."

"So that's why they call you a doctor, eh?" replied Cougar. At least her altered brain could still muster a Canadian accent.

Cougar looked down the row of now-empty cryogenic cubes, except for one at the very end with its lid still down. As she recalled, that sealed chamber belonged to Sergeant Kenny Childers, their maintenance specialist. Six cryo-cubes for their full crew, and only one still active.

"Everybody's awake except Kenny," noted Doctor Mercedes, when he saw her gazing down the aisle. "He's scheduled for reactivation next."

"Reactivation? You make us sound like machines. I notice I'm one of the last to join the party."

"We always save the troublemakers 'til last," he replied. "You and Kenny, that is."

"How about you?" asked Cougar. "You had five years to make lots of trouble."

"Which is exactly how I spent my time," he replied, squinting his eyes in a mischievous way, like he meant it.

"Well, thanks for taking care of me first. I know it wasn't in our original plan."

"Your brain may seem confused for quite a while. When you combine surgery with cryogenic sleep, I really don't know what you should expect. But you look no worse than the others. Expect to take a while to adapt to a normal diet."

Cougar sat on the cryo-bed looking at the doctor, unable to focus her attention on much of anything.

"It's probably how it feels when senility sets in," she muttered slowly in a purposefully muted tone.

"I just hope you remember where we're going, and how we'll get there," replied Mercedes. "You're the NavCom, after all."

"Is that what I am?" she asked. "Right now, I just know I'm a puking kleptomaniac who looks like shit."

◊ ◊ ◊ ◊ ◊ ◊

Chapter 3

## Near-Galactic Voyage

THE *CHALLENGER* MISSION WAS the first real galactic voyage, and even this fell far short of a trip across the Milky Way. Until now, flight to the nearest stars and their lifeless solar systems was the best that Earth could muster, even with fusion drives and the advent of Thomson-Jump technology. This would be the first mission striving to span a small portion of the Orion spur of the Milky Way's Sagittarius spiral arm, home of Earth and its sun. It would be a baby step across the galactic sea, but a bold voyage beyond the closest stars.

Prior to this, manned spacecraft had traveled a little over 10 light-years from Earth, far enough to encounter a variety of stellar systems with planets, all without intelligent life. Robotic spacecraft hadn't increased mankind's span, although these unmanned missions had been able to explore more thoroughly with their nearly ageless computerized components. Still, there was nothing in the 10-light-year radius that seemed capable of harboring intelligent life.

So far, these voyages to the nearby stars had been one-way trips to set up distant colonies in space. Most were assumed to have failed, and never heard from again. With the communication distance so great, it typically took more than a decade to receive a reply to the simplest message, so no one really knew whether any current colonies were self-sustaining. Still, there had never been a lack of eager volunteers, colonists willing to risk everything for a chance to do what no one else had ever done – establish a human existence on a planet outside our solar system. Maybe some of these colonies were actually flourishing, and were even now stepping out farther into the galactic void.

*Challenger*, from the very start, was a different type of mission. Named after an ill-fated spacecraft of the early era of space exploration, the ship was the first to employ cryogenic hibernation for extensive periods along with space tunneling jumps for stretches of up to 33 light-years. Both technologies had taken longer to develop than expected, or at least to perfect. With the onset of even minor irregularities, lives were lost, or crews simply never heard from again. And irregularities were the norm in space travel. Propel a spaceship far enough, and something would ultimately go wrong.

But the developers of *Challenger*, basing their efforts on improvements in cryogenics and the Thomson-Jump, were intent on defying death during cross-galactic flight. Naming the ship after a twentieth-century Space Shuttle that had blown itself to bits during launch, killing the entire crew, seemed a contradiction. Like the original *Challenger*, the new spaceship was crewed by a small contingent of spacefarers who were mostly along for the ride, since nearly everything was automated. But the ship's name was appropriate when one considered the we-must-learn attitude of the team that developed the new technologies required for a trans-galactic voyage.

*Challenger* was assigned a crew of six, all military aviation professionals who grew up in an era of pilotless fighters and bombers, computer war technology, and a business-like atmosphere seeming more like a global corporation than the traditional military. Like those colonists before them who left Earth never expecting to return, *Challenger's* crew was resolved to their fate. Their mission, although not technically one-way, had so many contingencies built in that the crew knew they had little chance of ever returning home. The primary goal was to travel to a planet 101 light-years away, hunt for intelligent life on this prospective world, and return to Earth to personally report the results. With the latest technologies in cryogenics, fusion drives, and Thomson-Jumps, this (theoretically) could be accomplished in a round-trip of forty Earth-years of aging for the crewmembers. Physically, that's how much older they would be when (if) they returned home. Thus, at least hypothetically, it would be possible for the crew to learn about a destination over a hundred light-years away in less than half the time it would take for a one-way communication signal to span the same distance. Einstein's theory of relativity didn't specifically forbid this untested theoretical result, but *Challenger's* financial developers didn't openly reveal some of the complications that were likely. While the money was flowing in, the public was quick to support back-of-the-envelope calculations as real rather than academic, all in an effort to learn more about the cosmos.

Captain Tina Brett, age 45 at the start of the journey, would be in her late 80's upon their theoretical return to Earth, a fate she didn't dwell on. After all, the average life expectancy of modern women was 97, while men statistically averaged 92. Tina Brett held the military rank of Lieutenant General in the Space Force of the North American Union, but her crew called her "Captain" because of her position as mission commander. Despite her air of authority, she was dainty in stature and delicately pretty, her lips lush and often brightly colored. Her short blond hair was soft and straight, lying close against her attractive face.

Captain Brett hailed from New England, where she grew up on a farm and attended the University of New Hampshire, using the school's ROTC program as her personal physical and psychological challenge. She graduated twenty-third in her class of 2,721 students. Since then, she'd learned how to concentrate.

Major Kim Lin, although only 31 years old, had already served on two solar system missions. As *Challenger's* engineering officer, he filled a position tied more to computer technology than the mechanical systems that were, for the most part, fully automated and self-repairing. Although he seemed to have no close friends, Kim's quiet personality and intense dedication to the mission made *Challenger's* crew feel comfortable with him.

Assisting Major Lin was Sergeant Kenneth Childers, maintenance specialist, age 27. Kenny was unofficially the ship's designated prankster. But he knew his spacecraft systems, and that was the reason he was aboard. Few spare parts were carried on a modern spaceship, so ongoing maintenance was his primary concern. Childers certainly knew his job, but off-duty he never seemed to have a serious side. Everyone liked to kid with Kenny.

Lieutenant Cougar Jensen, age 34, was the NavCom officer with the overhauled brain. She wore her dirty-blond hair short. Her thin athletic body with small breasts made it common for new acquaintances to consider her "cute," while simultaneously wondering about her sexuality. Her low rank as an officer was because she had spent most of her post-college life as an Earth-based commercial air carrier pilot, transferring to the Space Force of the North American Union two years prior to the launch of *Challenger*. In recent decades, flying was so automated that commercial pilots merely monitored the aircraft systems and navigated and communicated through computer interfaces, which is where Cougar shined. Now that they were out of the Earth's radius of communication, the "Com" part of her job would be with any alien intelligence they might discover or unexpected colonial spacecraft they might encounter. Cougar's "Nav" function would be her primary job, although even that was highly automated, except for occasional complications that could always be expected.

The last two members of the crew were both medical experts, which showed the thrust of the ship's composition: two pilots and leaders (Tina and Cougar), two mechanical experts (Kim and Kenny), and two medical wizards. Doctor Donald Mercedes, with his renowned lack of personality, led the medical team as the shipboard physician. He was 42 at the start of the mission, taller than the rest of the crew, prematurely bald, rather handsome, and meticulous about his professional appearance. He aged five years while the rest of the crew was in hibernation, so he would be pushing the standard male lifespan if they returned to Earth on schedule. Mercedes held the military rank of major, but his shipboard title was "Doctor." Although generally despised by the crew (except Cougar, who found him "interesting"), they all agreed he was the best choice for the job. Don Mercedes knew as much about all areas of medicine as anyone else on Earth, maybe more. Health concerns were on the top of the list when the crew considered essential items they'd need to control, so they universally accepted his questionable charisma.

If Don Mercedes was at the bottom of *Challenger's* crew personality gauge, Sergeant Timothy Hammer, age 43, was near the top, only exceeded by Captain Tina Brett. As a technohealth specialist, he was adored (and occasionally bribed) as the crew's key to a robust day-to-day routine. Not only was he the ship's expert on the all-important cryogenic cubes, he doled out a host of pills that seemed to cure almost any ailment, including many that were more psychological than physical. His personality meshed with the rest of the crew textbook-perfect. Everyone liked Tim.

This six-member crew was small compared to former spaceships. All of the shipboard systems were automated, so the crew's job was to attend to the unexpected (Captain and NavCom), maintain the status quo (engineering officer and maintenance specialist), and take care of themselves (physician and technohealth specialist). Sustaining life aboard the starship took considerable space and sophistication, so a small crew was what was needed. The rest of the spacecraft, in order to get to its destination, was huge by design.

Cougar had occasionally reflected on the crew composition. Was the female concentration in the command area – Cougar considered her NavCom responsibilities closely related to Captain Brett's leadership role – by chance or choice? And why did each specialty (leadership, maintenance, and medical) consist of two individuals rather than one? Environmental space was minimal and demanding, so why include six crewmembers when three would seem to fill the requirements? Her conclusion was that redundancy was one of the what-if's of the long mission. What if one of the two maintenance experts died, or what if something happened to Mercedes or Halmer, or to her or Brett? It seemed only logical that the mission planning team must have built this consideration into the crew composition. And maybe females were simply better at leadership decisions on long voyages. There had been two well-documented colonial failures involving male leaders who lost control of their personnel before even reaching their destination.

And what of the sexual scenarios? The project development team must have considered the possible situations. All six of them were single, although Halmer and Mercedes had been previously married. It made sense that leaving a spouse behind would be unacceptable to personal psyche, but what about their decades together in space, and the whole concept of sexual relationships among the crew? Had anyone really thought this out? Cougar, for one, had consciously ignored it. The mission was her opportunity of a lifetime, and sexual confrontations (or whatever might occur when it came to sexual clashes) seemed a small price to pay.

Another question originally tugging at the back of Cougar's old brain involved the split of the crew into four males and two females. What was that all about? Maybe *Challenger's* project team had determined (as Cougar had surmised) that several members of the crew were homosexual. Cougar thought Kenny Childers might be gay, and she already knew about Tina Brett's bisexuality (Tina and Cougar were bunk-mates and close friends). But that skewed the numbers even worse, making her the only heterosexual female with at least three raging males. Hopefully, the project team knew more than she did.

It didn't take long for the issue of sex to come to the forefront, just like in millions of similar undocumented instances that influenced human history.

## Chapter 4

### Donut Holes

"You're looking better, Kenny," said Cougar to the maintenance specialist over a cup of coffee. "Being last out of the cryo-chamber means it'll take you a while to catch up with the rest of us. There's plenty of time."

"I suppose so, Lieutenant," replied Kenny, still shaky after a full 24 hours out of the chamber. "I wish I hadn't been the last to wake up."

"Somebody had to, although I thought you outranked Sergeant Halmer. Maybe the Captain just likes him better."

Cougar laughed, to make sure Kenny didn't take her seriously. Sergeant Kenny Childers gave her a serious stare, and then his mouth eased into a gentle smile.

"It's just the way the operational order was written," he replied. "There's really no rhyme or reason, I suppose. Heck you were next to last and you're second in line to Captain Brett."

That seemed to make him feel better, and he gripped his coffee cup more steadily, raised it for a brief sip, and set it back down with a new frown on his face.

"Tastes terrible," he said. "Nothing tastes good yet."

"It'll take time, Kenny. I had the dry heaves for two days. Now look how pretty I am."

Kenny laughed, and that too made him look a bit better. It would take time, as volumes of research back on Earth had proven repeatedly. There was no quick fix for post-cryogenic rejuvenation.

"Everybody else is doing okay?" asked Kenny.

"Sure. Everything's back to normal, or as normal as it can be while speeding through space a light-year from home. Even Doctor Whacko seems okay, although he must be pissed by staying awake all the time we were asleep."

"Seems like it worked rather well for you. Brain surgery must not be easy under these conditions. You're looking good."

"You mean pretty, don't you?" joked Cougar.

Kenny laughed, and seemed to blush, which appeared to be an unusual reaction, since Cougar was rather sure he was gay.

"Sure, you're pretty," replied Kenny, now looking more composed.

"Actually, I'm still feeling rather weird, like I'm in this body of mine, but still in a fog."

"The fog of war," kidded Kenny.

"More like the fog of peace. Nobody to fight with around here, thank goodness. To put it another way, my mind seems slow. I keep striving to remember things I'll probably never comprehend. It's all there, basically, but pretty disjointed at the moment."

"Maybe he gave you a monkey's brain. Do you crave bananas and want to scratch your armpits?"

"Very funny, Sergeant," laughed Cougar. "I'm pretty foggy, but not in a primate sort of way. Besides, where would Mercedes find a monkey brain? There aren't any extra organic parts sitting on the shelf around here, primate or human. On this trip, if something can't be fixed or manufactured in the Fabricator, we'll need to live without it."

"What little I know of Mercedes, I wouldn't want to trust him with my life," replied Kenny. "Maybe I'll need him some day, but I hope he lightens up by then."

"Lightens up? It must be pretty hard to lighten up when he knows everybody considers him a grump. I actually kind of like the guy, especially since he saved my life."

"A new life with a monkey brain," replied Kenny. "Or maybe a cougar brain. How'd you ever get that nickname, anyway?"

"It's not a nickname, Kenny. It's my real name. My mom and dad are real outdoorsy types. Me too. What's wrong with mountain lions?"

"Nothing. So I guess if he gave you a cougar brain, you wouldn't even know the difference."

One thing for sure about this crew, thought Cougar – they weren't going to get hung up over rank consciousness. There wouldn't be much pomp and ceremony on this voyage, judging by what she'd experienced so far. Which was fine with her.

\* \* \* \* \*

When Cougar started her first shift on the bridge, the only workstation open was at the bow, which was her normal location. Captain Brett was at her console at the rear, with the other two side-by-side stations in the middle occupied by Doctor Mercedes and Major Lin, the engineering officer. The workstations were exactly the same in every respect, right down to the model of side-table electronic tablets and the cushy high-backed swivel chairs. A conference table with two additional computer terminals sat behind the Captain, used by the two enlisted members of the crew when they needed working space. Today this area was vacant, with only the four officers on the bridge.

The workstations were a fluid concept. When Kenny Childers, the maintenance specialist, needed access to the more powerful bridge computers, he'd slide into whatever officer station might be vacant at the time. So Cougar might occasionally end up at another location, a form of musical chairs. Even the Captain's helm wasn't sacred. If everything else was full, and Captain Brett was absent, a crewmember needing a workstation would slip into her seat, and Tina Brett would temporarily use the conference table until her station was vacated. Unless, of course, she or another officer needed critical information stored only in the main bridge workstations. Only then would an officer consider bumping an enlisted sergeant from his seat.

This worked without a single instance of concern, for the crew worked together that closely, even Doctor Mercedes in this regard. Until Cougar signed in with her user name (NavCom) and password (N48968G, the registration number of her personal hovercraft back on Earth), the workstation was exactly like all the others. Once logged on, however, the navigation and communication suite filled her screen.

Someone back home must have worried long and hard about this arrangement, before finally authorizing the electronic interface. Workstation duplication promoted operational simplification and was user-friendly in its security design. It stood to reason that access to Cougar's files would be needed if anything happened to her, although her password would authenticate only if it matched the one she had stored in the ship's master computer. If her overhauled brain suddenly hemorrhaged, the Captain could quickly retrieve her password to assure the navigation function never missed a beat. The fact there was any kind of security at all made Cougar occasionally reflect on what the ship's designers had taken into account when they set up the bridge in the first place.

"NavCom" typed Cougar. Then "N48968G." For a few moments, she paused, thinking of her old hovercraft and life back on Earth, an existence abandoned like a terminally ill patient who tries to wrap up her life when she realizes the end is near. Her beloved HoverSmart was no longer sitting in her garage, sold to someone who probably could never love this wonderful vehicle properly. Her strato-apartment in Miami was now occupied by someone else, a structure climate-hardened only a few years ago in anticipation of a flooded topography that was soon to transform coastal Florida into a Venice-like landscape. Her friends from the Space Force of the North American Union had been left behind, as if she had died. Reluctantly, she had relinquished memories of material things she cherished and people she loved – all far behind her now, in both space and time.

When she snapped back to reality, the display in front of her was already lit up, a large screen segmented into four equal-sized rectangles: "Position" was the label in the upper left, with a map overlay depicting their location in space; "Planned Maneuvers" read the upper right, with a list of three upcoming events requiring her attention. The bottom two screens were totally blank except for their titles: "Nav Scenarios" and "Communication."

Even after being away from the "office" for five years, there wasn't any pressing business waiting for her, so she moved the cursor around the screen, checking what few details were displayed. The position map looked like she expected. The spacecraft was now 0.8 light-years from Earth, still a fraction of the distance to the nearest star. When Captain Tina Brett came out of the cryo-chamber four days earlier, she had transmitted their first message home after five years of inactivity. Cougar's first task today would be to send the technical details back to Earth, including precise position data and parameters involving their flight plan. It seemed a mute point, with Earth now so far away that any return message wouldn't be received for nearly two years. Consider it a formality, thought Cougar, and treat it seriously, even though it seemed monkey-brained.

The position display was as she had expected, or at least within reason. A yellow circle represented the ship's predicted location based on their last known position, uploaded to the nav system just before they nodded off to sleep. Here in space, the only way to acquire an accurate position was from the stellar background, an advanced form of celestial navigation. The interesting part of the nav parameters was that the stellar background was changing ever so slightly as the spacecraft traveled through space. Back in the solar system, astronauts had never detected any movement of the background stars. Here, traveling across the galactic sea (or at least across the galactic arm), the nearest stars were subject to a slight parallax value. The computerized system, of course, took this into account in its navigational calculations, and projected a yellow circle representing the probable position of the ship since the last known fix.

Space navigators from centuries gone by referred to this as the "probable position spread," or more commonly these days as the "donut hole" or simply the "donut." So there was the expected circle, larger than Cougar had ever seen it before, since no position fix had been obtained for five years. The diameter of the hole equated to the anticipated inaccuracy of their position, based on a number of factors, many of which were not totally understood by anyone. Back in the days when spacecraft were first leaving the solar system, it was quickly learned that predicted positions were just that – predictions, with a bell-shaped curve representing the probability of being at any particular point in space.

In the early Twenty-First Century, Pioneer 10 and 11, the first robotic spacecraft to exit the solar system, deviated farther off course than their own designated donuts, and scientists were perplexed. Something seemed to be slowing these space vessels down more than expected as they departed the sun's sphere of influence. In the case of the Pioneer spacecraft, it was eventually discovered that thermal radiation pressure had not been taken into account properly, and introduction of that revised variable into the trajectory solved the dilemma.

Two centuries later, donut holes still possessed a credible size that wasn't entirely understood. Thermal radiation was now included in the trajectory computations, but other anomalies occasionally entered the picture. Technical experts thought the diameter of the holes would decrease substantially over time, once the forces of physics were more thoroughly understood. But even now, after journeys to the nearest stars, scientists were still scratching their heads, unable to reduce the donut even close to the size of a point in space. It was one of those unknowns making the actions of navigators still a bit of an art, tempered with a huge dose of celestial mechanics.

It took Cougar little more than a flick of the cursor and a tap of the touch-screen to launch the first navigational update in a half-decade. Within only a few seconds, the ship's giant main computer spit out the answer by placing a bright yellow pinpoint on the screen in front of her. It sat on the bottom edge of the donut hole, partially obliterated by the arc of the circle. Surprise!

Cougar leaned back in her chair, pushing her body into the soft fabric, where the zero-G belt constrained her from floating away. This was their first day in zero-G after the few days they spent in ship-standard 0.7-G conditions after coming out of hibernation. Their stay in normal gravity had been brief, since they were already preparing for their first Thomson-Jump, which required non-rotational conditions for the ship. The weightless condition always took awhile to get used to.

She took a deep breath, and then studied the results in front of her. She'd expected their position to lie well within the donut, although the nav computer's display was designed to accept any result that didn't violate the span of the hole. Still, the outer regions of the circle were reserved for anomalies that built up over time, amplified by the many unpredictable conditions that could occur in outer space – small meteor strikes, unexpected concentrations of interstellar gas, and a multitude of routine space encounters over a span of years. But Tina had briefed the crew as soon as they woke up – there had been no recorded anomalies. That didn't rule out unexpected variables not built into the flight plan, including unknown force fields not yet discovered by science.

Still, even taking all of these unknowns into account, Cougar stared at the bright dot intersecting the bottom edge of the donut, slightly off to the left side. She'd never seen anything like it before. Then again, no one had ever been this far from Earth in all of history.

Before reporting the results to Tina or including it in her positional details message for Earth, Cougar decided to run an alternate computation to be more certain of the results. Rather than use the automated system, she selected the "Three Star" position fix using the semi-automated sextant. Instead of allowing the computer to select the best available stars for the determination of their position, she'd personally choose three favorably positioned targets. Normally, the fully automated computation was more accurate, since it took into account the angular spread between the selected stars, which provided a more exact measurement. In this case, Cougar would pick the stars herself, providing an alternate computation that should show their position in an almost identical location. In such cases, the fully automated computation was always more accurate, but today she wasn't so sure.

Cougar scrolled down the list of stars, picking three bright ones she could easily identify from the bow windows. Her panoramic view from the front was the best in the ship, which was why the navigator's normal workstation was located here. Although most of the time the ship was slowly spinning around its long axis to create artificial gravity, today the crew enjoyed the majestic fixed view. They would remain weightless right up to the first Thomson-Jump.

This first jump seemed rushed, considering the long-range voyage they were only now beginning, but it was according to their flight plan. The mission scenario considered cryogenic hibernation and Thomson-Jumps still somewhat experimental, so Earth wanted to get the first of each behind them quickly. If there were problems (other than the worst-case scenario of a premature end to the mission), they could still adjust before the point-of-no-return, the spot in space where it would take too long to return to Earth with their limited fuel and environmental resources. Once beyond that point, they were committed to their destination, where they expected to find adequate water to turn into hydrogen for nuclear fuel and oxygen for breathing – even enough to return home. Thus, both the initial cryogenic period and the first Thomson-Jump were crowded together, with more leisurely scheduling anticipated for the remainder of the journey.

From Cougar's front-seat view, she could see over a third of the sky. Since her station was located somewhat rearward and outward from the ship's true bow, she couldn't see what was below her, and looking back more than 90 degrees to either side was awkward. Still, everyone called her workstation "the bow," although the real front of the ship was nearly a hundred meters away.

The spaceship was pencil-shaped rearward from the crew module, which was egg-shaped and wider than the rest of the ship. The module was intentionally broad, with the living and working areas (which included the bridge) spread around the periphery of the egg's shell. This allowed their 0.7-G standard to be produced by slow rotation of the crew module. Without the wide profile, an uncomfortably fast rotation would be needed, producing disconcerting visual cues when the bridge's bow shutters were open.

Atmospheric drag for such a design would have been insurmountable, so the entire ship was constructed in low Earth orbit, a process that consumed over four years. All of the interrelated modules were built on Earth, and then lifted into orbit by huge old-fashioned non-fusion rockets that relied on a combination of liquid and solid boosters. The ship's crew shuttled back and forth from Earth, continually involved in the spaceship's in-orbit assembly. If they were to fly this behemoth vessel across the galactic arm, they'd need to be intimately familiar with the details of its construction.

Even with the crew module's large silhouette, its slow rotation was easily noticeable and sometimes unsettling. When Cougar used her sextant for celestial navigation, she found it was best to limit her star shots to periods when there was no rotation, just prior to cryogenic sessions or before Thomson Jumps, when zero-G was the standard configuration.

The fusion reactor was at the end of the narrow cylinder that extended more than two kilometers behind, so it didn't obstruct

Cougar's observation of the stars. Depending on where the ship was aimed, the best views were up and to the sides. On this voyage, the nose was pointed towards the Constellation of Hercules, so she chose her target stars accordingly.

First she selected Altair in the SkySearch function, and the semi-automated sextant swung towards the star. She knew her constellations well enough to know the instrument was operating properly, and it stopped with the crosshair view filling the Nav Scenarios rectangle of the display in front of her. There was no need to adjust the sextant's position at all, since the crosshairs covered the star perfectly.

Next she selected Arcturus from the list, and the drive gears rotated to the right, towards the opposite side of the sky, slowing and then finally stopping on the bright orange star. Once again, the crosshairs were so perfectly aligned that she did nothing to override the position. Now she selected her last star, Deneb. The sextant moved back to the left, stopping at the bright point of light. This time the crosshairs were not perfectly aligned on the star, although so close it seemed inconsequential. With a gentle touch, Cougar used her joystick to drive the crosshairs directly on top of the star, needing several tries before she could improve on the computer's original optical positioning.

It would have made her feel triumphant to find this small variation were it not for the fact that she knew Deneb was closer to Altair than was normally considered acceptable for a "Three Star" position fix. With these two stars so close together, the accuracy of the ship's position would be slightly compromised. But in this case she was looking for an alternate computation, even if it was less exact. Maybe she could find something wrong with the automated computation.

The last step in determining their exact position was to select the "Fix Position Now" button on her Nav Scenarios screen. When she touched the button, the alternate position appeared almost instantly on the map at the top left of her console. An orange dot sat right on top of the bright yellow spot, indicating the two computations agreed, with no discernable difference. Both dots proclaimed they were located right on the edge of their ship's predicted position. Or were they?

With her screen resolution set to normal, it was impossible to tell if the two dots were right on the outer edge of the donut hole. This ring was displayed with significant diameter, since it was a rare occurrence (never in Cougar's experience) when an actual position fix would be this far astray. By zooming in, it would be easy to tell whether their position was on the ring or slightly inside or outside of it. Of course, they had to be either on or inside the ring.

Cougar hit the zoom button, and then punched it again, to make the donut hole enlarge to fill nearly the whole width of the screen. The ring was now more sharply portrayed – a brilliant finely-defined yellow arc. At this viewing scale, the yellow and orange dots were separated by a small but noticeable gap. Both were well below the expected position and slightly to the left. Both dots were outside the ring.

*****

"Captain, NavCom has a position update for you."

Although the distance between their workstations was only 10 meters, Cougar used her headset microphone to transmit her request for the Captain's attention. When it came in over Tina's workstation speaker, she put on her headset to keep their conversation from disturbing the others on the bridge.

"Go ahead, Coug," replied Tina.

"A close look at our position shows something you wouldn't expect. In fact, we're out of the prescribed limits, mostly south of our expected location, but also slightly to the west. I had to zoom in to detect it, but we're outside the donut border. Take a look."

The image from Cougar's display now appeared on Tina's screen, zoomed to the magnification that clearly showed the aberration in position. The directional indicators used in astro-navigation were a convenience, since there were no true directions in space. Since they were headed towards the constellation of Hercules, it was referred to as true north. Earth, behind them, was south, with east and west off to each side. A fix notably south of their expected location (the bottom of the screen) meant they were short of their predicted location. Since the dot was also slightly to the left, it meant they were off course "to the west."

"Can't be, can it?" said Tina.

"I've never seen it before, but technically we could be right on the ring under conditions involving unexpected anomalies over such a long period. But never outside, at least according to theory."

"I guess all bets on theory are off," replied Tina. "Have you tried verifying the calculation by going semi-automatic?"

"Been there, done that. A three-star calculation shows almost exactly the same – here, I'll send it to you now. It's displayed for you as an orange dot." Tina's revised screen, including the new orange dot, flickered into view immediately. "I'll try some more three-star calculations using targets with better geometry, but it looks pretty conclusive. What are the chances my first three-star shot would be that close to the fully automated version but still outside the ring, eh?"

"Never heard of it," replied Tina. "Go ahead and do a few more semi-automated fixes, just to make sure we're covering our ass."

"And who are we covering our ass from?" laughed Cougar.

"Just the six of us, dangling out here in space," replied Tina. "I'll let the rest of the gang know as soon as we confirm the anomaly, but don't transmit your position message to Earth quite yet. Let's make sure we're a hundred percent sure before getting them excited. After all, what can they do about it?"

"Well, I guess they can mull it over, and then send back a recommendation we'll receive years from now. By then we'll be through our first Thomson-Jump, thirty-three more light-years from here. It kinda' sounds like were on our own, don't you think?"

"We've been on our own ever since we went to sleep. Maybe we need to find a bigger donut."

## Chapter 5

## Thomson-Jump

LATER THE SAME DAY, COUGAR asked Tina to rotate the ship 50 degrees clockwise, so she would be able to view an area of the sky with a better spread of bright targets. Although she could use fainter stars for a position fix, she wanted to eliminate the possibility of misidentifying them, since she was more confident with the brightest stars. Cougar was well trained in her constellations (although she still struggled with the Earth's southern hemisphere), but she preferred to stick with what she knew best.

Rotating a ship this big in the manual mode was no simple task, and Tina worked at it with Cougar's help on the checklists. After a series of short rocket thrusts, nearly the full 50 degrees of rotation was achieved, and then they used precisely-timed quick pulses in the opposite direction to bring the rotation to a complete stop.

When the ship was stable again, Cougar began another three-star fix, selecting two of the same stars – Deneb and Arcturus – since they were spread by nearly 60 degrees. The third target was Regulus, farther to the right, making a nearly-equilateral triangle, which should provide results nearly as accurate as the fully automated procedure.

When the new position appeared on her navigational map, it popped up as an orange point of light with labeled "A2" for "Alternate #2." Simultaneously, her previous three-star fix received it's own label, now designated "A1." All three positions (the original yellow automated one, along with A1 and A2) overlaid each other so close they seemed to merge into one. Tina had called up Cougar's map for display at her own workstation. When she saw A2 pop up, she muttered a soft but intent "Damn it!"

While the ship was rotated in this new orientation, Cougar took the time to select three more stars, and watched as an agonizing "A3" overlaid the other fixes with barely a bit of space between them. If Tina was watching as A3 suddenly arrived on her screen, she didn't say anything this time. Ever since the first yellow point was displayed, neither she nor Cougar held much hope by adding new fixes to the navigational data.

They simply accepted their position as real, and didn't talk about it again until they were back in their room that night. Cougar bunked above Tina in their small personal cubicle, big enough for the two beds, two chairs (one soft and comfortable, the other a straight-backed rocker), a table for two mini-tablets, and a mirror hinged on a medicine cabinet. In a small adjacent area sat their toilet, sink, and shower. It had been only in the past few decades that spacefarers had the luxury of running water. With artificial gravity in the normally-spinning structure of *Challenger*, dry-showers and suction toilets had become a frustration of the past, revisited only when the ship wasn't rotating. Every drop of water was recycled, a commodity as precious as their valuable pile of fusion fuel.

"Not much to do about it," said Tina. "Maneuvering back on course shouldn't be a big deal."

"Just a little extra time, that's all. I'd suggest we delay our course correction until after the Thomson-Jump. Being short of our expected position this much is mighty perplexing, but there's certainly nothing we can do about it, since we're already at maximum continuous cruise speed. Although the off-course deviation is of concern, it's less than our speed-line error. If you think the donut ring is big now, wait 'til we make the first jump. By design, we'll be trading a precise position for instantaneous transfer to our new location. For a 33-light-year jump, the error radius is plus or minus three one-hundredths of a light-year, which is huge compared to what we're looking at now."

"But our little error will be magnified by the jump," countered Tina, playing devil's advocate.

"Sure, but the position deviation from the jump might push us back on course, so we may as well take the chance. It's possible we could be more precisely aligned when we come out of the jump. Who knows?"

"Exactly the point," said Tina, in her normal consider-all-scenarios mode. "Who knows? If this was Las Vegas, I'd say let it go, and see what happens. The odds are as much in our favor as against us. Unless, of course, you believe in luck. Then we definitely should go with your suggestion."

"Six of one, half a dozen of the other," replied Cougar. "Luck doesn't enter into the equation during nav calculations. Or does it?"

"I'd never admit it. But just to be sure, let's make the jump without a course correction, and see if we can make a case for Lady Luck."

"It's really no big deal either way," said Cougar. "Even if we end up a bit farther off course, we can correct. It's just extra time, but that begs the real question, doesn't it?"

"Meaning, our fuel reserves?"

"Partly that," replied Cougar. "It'll use up some of our reserves if we lose, but I don't see it sucking up more fuel than we need. After all, we haven't made a single course correction yet, and we've been underway for almost six years. No, I'm referring to the bigger question – With all our computerized gismos and the vast applied knowledge of the *Challenger* project team over a period of three decades, why are we so far off course?"

\* \* \* \* \*

THE NEXT DAY, TINA spent most of her time at her workstation, reviewing the automated portion of the ship's log, looking for any anomalies that might have caused their excursion outside the donut. Just as she had reported to her crew, there were no obvious events that might have caused the deviation. But an unexpected slowing in speed by only a fraction of a percent would be enough to put them outside the speed-line computation, which could account for the difference. The recorded data was straightforward – their velocity had not deviated from 0.13 SOL to an accuracy of five decimal points, so they shouldn't be south of their expected position. The slight deviation to the west, since it didn't violate normal expectations, was less of concern regarding the "why" of the puzzle. But their short-of-anticipated position in space was strange, and would eventually have to be corrected, whether by a "lucky" Thomson-Jump or through use of reserve fuel burned in the ship's thrusters.

Two weeks after the donut hole surprise, without a single course correction since leaving the solar system, they made their first Thomson-Jump.

\* \* \* \* \*

In 2153, Efren Thomson discovered something even better than the long-fantasized warp drive, although it took fifty more years to perfect it enough to be installed in a spacecraft. In 2207, a "jump drive" had been successfully tested, using short hops inside the solar system. Human crews were seemingly unaffected by the huge power surges necessary to instantaneously transition from here to there in zero seconds. Of course, that violated Einstein's theory of relativity, allowing nothing to exceed the speed of light – unless the spacecraft that appeared near Saturn wasn't the same object that disappeared from an orbit around the Earth. In fact, the Thomson-Jump Drive was more of a time machine than a space vehicle, nearly simultaneously transforming and transferring an existing spaceship to a place far-far away, where it reappeared as a new ship in the old vessel's clothing, human crew and all. Extensive evaluation of the crewmembers, when they returned to Earth, verified they were pretty much the same as when they left, although technically completely different. Humans were basically the same after the Thomson-Jump as before.

In 2219 and 2221, reportedly, there had been two successful Thomson-Jumps of over a light-year each during two separate missions to nearby stars. "Reportedly" was added to the historical record, since the disappearance of both ships was thoroughly documented, and reappearance at the expected jump location was verified, but communications with both vessels of colonists was never established again. This became the reluctantly-accepted norm for one-way space missions in the Twenty-Third Century.

Short-range jumps were thoroughly documented and pronounced effective and safe, and long-range jumps seemed to work as well. The *Challenger* was the first attempt to utilize Thomson-Jump technology to its hypothetical limit of 33.1 light-years. In theory, a jump of 33 light-years should be no different than a leap from Earth to Saturn. The computations that conclusively verified this range limitation were so solid that Tina and her crew bought into the theoretical limit, although none of them really understood the math.

Thus, the mission profile called for departing Earth under their fusion drive's acceleration to 0.31 SOL (their maximum cruise speed under ordinary conditions), followed six months later by cryogenic sleep for five years, followed by less than a month to rejuvenate their bodies, followed by a 33 light-year Thomson-Jump, repeated on-

and-on to their destination. It would be a cycle of cryogenic periods interspersed with Thomson-Jumps, plus a few years here and there for deceleration at their destination. And maybe even a trip home.

As they prepared for their first Thomson-Jump, the ship's officers occupied all four bridge workstations. Sergeants Tim Hammer and Kenny Childers sat buckled in at the conference table behind the forward stations. Lieutenant Cougar Jensen called out the checklist items from her bow location, while Captain Tina Brett readied the ship for the jump at her seat at the rear console. Dr. Don Mercedes occupied his normal position in front of Tina, with nothing to do. Next to him, Major Kim Lin monitored the ship's systems, knowing this was the most critical time for something to go wrong. A mechanical failure now would be no less expected than any other time, but the results could be disastrous. Everything had to be perfect to survive a 33-light-year Thomson-Jump. But if it was survivable, it would instantaneously move them a third of the way to their destination.

"Fusion drive," said Cougar as she read the checklist.

This was the ninety-third item on the final list, with twenty-seven still to go. They'd been in their seats for over two hours, with some of the earlier items on the checklist (such as pressurization changes in the ship) taking lengthy periods to complete. They had spent the previous week running their ship-securing checklist in anticipation of the maneuver.

"Fusion drive is locked," replied Tina, as she touched the icon labeled "FD Safe," and watched it change from red to green.

"Environmental systems," stated Cougar, trying to keep a professional voice throughout the procedures.

"Minimized. Both scrubbers on standby," replied Tina.

On and on they went, until halfway through the remaining items, Tina turned to Kim Lin for assistance.

"Kim, should I lock the hydraulic ATM in override, or leave it on standby?"

"Standby is probably best," he replied. "Just in case there's a prolonged delay before the jump. The hydraulics will come back up to pressure quicker in standby position, if something bad happens."

"Heaven forbid something bad," replied Tina. "Okay, Cougar, hydraulics is set on standby."

One of the many unknowns of a Thomson-Jump was the delay before the ship's relocation actually occurred. It was a basic extension of Heisenberg's Uncertainty Principle. In this case, a jump might be delayed as much as much as three hours before the actual relocation occurred, really more of a plod than a leap. When a jump was initiated, it was impossible to determine whether it would occur immediately or hours later.

There was a way to speed the process, but emergency jumps were reserved for urgent situations, since the tradeoff for a guaranteed quick jump was a position inaccuracy at the other end that was nearly doubled. Even with a normal Thomson-Jump, the position error (which increased with the distance spanned) was as much as 0.02 light-years for a 33 light-year jump. So you couldn't aim for an spot near a targeted object, because you could easily smash into it instead. The coordinates set into the Thomson-Jump time machine had to honor the 0.02 light-year error radius, which meant slogging onward at normal fusion drive speeds to your destination for another few months after the transition was complete. In this case, the target was in the middle of nowhere, so the error radius was a mute point, but it would rear its ugly head when they approached their final destination.

"Anybody got anything else?" inquired Tina, when she finally completed the checklist.

The bridge sat in silence for a few seconds, and then Tina reached forward for the final touch-screen icon marked "Activate Jump."

"Hold on to your hats," she said. "We're going for a ride. Just don't know exactly when."

After activating the jump, the six crewmembers sat in their ergonomic chairs waiting for the interruption to the ship's power, the only sure sign the transition was beginning. Nothing happened for almost 2 hours, so everyone turned to their station computers to play games or catch up on some unfinished data entries they'd been putting off for days.

When the bridge lights started to blink, Cougar was the first to respond: "Ready, set, go! See you on the other side, eh?"

\* \* \* \* \*

THE OTHER SIDE WAS REMARKABLY like the side they left. The blinking of the overhead lights continued for several minutes, but without any unusual vibrations within the ship or any feeling of movement. The spacecraft never totally lost electrical power, nor did their display panels lose their images. But when things settled down, all the workstation displays automatically rebooted in an attempt to retrieve the masses of data that had suddenly changed. In Cougar's case, her four segmented panels went blank almost simultaneously, and came back to life one at a time, a process that took a few minutes. As soon as the position map was displayed, she notified Tina, even before digesting the details.

"New position, Captain," said Cougar over the common headset channel they were all monitoring. "We're within the error radius expected, at least at first glance. Let's see... Looks like the original donut error is about the same. Still out of limits south, although only slightly. And displaced a tad to the west, just like before. I'd say we didn't gain or lose on this one."

"Which goes to prove," replied Tina.

"Proves what?" asked Doctor Mercedes, expressing an unusual interest in what the leadership team was talking about.

"Oh, just something Coug and I were talking about awhile ago. It seems luck is neither for or against us when it comes to getting rid of the position error we found after our cryogenic period."

"As spoken by one of those who got to sleep," replied Mercedes.

He didn't sound mad, only joking about his five lost years. Which made Cougar take note. Doctor Mercedes seemed completely neutral regarding his mission-imposed aging caused by her brain surgery, and it didn't exactly mess with his withdrawn personality. Before the surgery, although Cougar never detested the doctor, she remembered him as more antagonistic and certainly more confrontational. Since the cryogenic sleep period, he seemed more of a team player, after having given up five years of his life unexpectedly. You'd think he'd at least complain about it.

"Coug, take a three-star shot as soon as you can," said Tina. "Let me know how it correlates with the new data."

"Roger, Captain. I'll get right on it."

The ship was now 34 light-years from Earth, most of that distance spanned in an instant. They were now slightly more than a third of the way to their destination, an obscure planet slightly larger than Earth that had inspired scientists for the past hundred years. A mix of rock and liquid water covered the planet, and it was the only object other than Earth known to be producing generous amounts of oxygen on its own. After centuries of fruitless searching, maybe there was intelligent life somewhere else in this galaxy. If so, *Challenger* was equipped to find it.

## Chapter 6

## **Bedside Manner**

"Hey, girlfriend, this has been quite a day."

Cougar always felt uncomfortable when Tina called her "girlfriend," although it was an obvious understatement. As the only females aboard *Challenger*, they had bonded early in their training. Even among the other crewmembers, they talked to each other informally, throwing in an occasional "Captain" or "Lieutenant" for good measure. More often, especially in the privacy of their quarters, it was "Tina" and "Coug."

Cougar was a bit uncomfortable with everything since her awakening from the 5-year hibernation. "Fogged" is how she described it. Although her frontal lobe pain was fully cured, and her hallucinations were gone, her mind felt dulled, a more general feeling than a specific malady. She retained all of her normal mental capabilities, including both short-term and long-term memory. She privately tested her mental math acuity, always an important aptitude for aviators and navigators at all levels. None of her mental capacity seemed reduced in any way, but still there was the all-encompassing fog that lurked in the background, as if she had been changed in some way that wasn't evident to others or even herself.

Her attitude towards Tina, for example, had drifted in various directions since her cryogenic sleep. Even during training for the mission, it was obvious Tina had a sensual interest in her – those occasional prolonged hugs when they celebrated success in a training exercise, or the brief touch of fingers when they stood side-by-side with the rest of the crew at an early morning briefing. None of that bothered Cougar. In fact, it was an aspect of Tina she enjoyed, poised on the gratifying border of a sister she'd never had and a sexual yearning she'd never experienced.

Ever since their first close contact during their mission training in Virginia, Tina had been direct and to the point about her sexuality. Cougar even remembered her exact words: "So, I suppose you've figured out that I'm bisexual," Tina had said matter-of-factly one night, after an intense session on the obstacle course. They were both comfortable with it, and sometimes it provided an interesting topic to pursue when they had the privacy to discuss such things, a calming ice-breaker of sorts, since they both had grown to accept their relationship as it was.

"It still makes you nervous when I call you 'girlfriend,' doesn't it?" said Tina.

"Oh, a bit. Maybe I can't decide whether I love it or hate it."

"Because I'm bisexual?" replied Tina.

"No, that's not a problem. Everything's fine," said Cougar with a sense of edginess she knew was obvious, although she didn't understand it herself. Maybe it was her brain still trying to settle down.

"Not a problem for you, or not a problem in general?" asked Tina.

"Both. You know that I'm not bisexual or lesbian, but I enjoy the closeness we have, so that's not something that's difficult for me. Heck, on-and-off, I'm on the verge of asexual, if that makes any sense."

Cougar always found it enjoyable to verbally spar with Tina, so maybe that's what she needed tonight. Anything to forget about the fog.

"A straight asexual gal? Sort of makes sense," kidded Tina.

"Well, it's not like I'm neutral on Tuesdays and Thursdays, and straight the rest of the week, but I'll certainly admit to being a bit fucked up."

"Though not literally," said Tina, letting a smile cross her pouty rose-tinted lips.

"No, not literally," replied Cougar, attempting to maintain a semblance of seriousness.

"Not much different than me," said Tina meekly. "I like men, too. It's just that I sometimes like women more than men. Actually, I can get along without a sexual relationship, as long as I can maintain strong friendships like ours. So I guess you could call me a bit asexual, too."

"I'll never tell," kidded Cougar.

"Actually, I'm not as worried about you as I am with the rest of the crew. As I see it, one of our biggest problems during our mission will involve how we all handle sexual encounters. As your mission commander, I can't think of anything worse than a battle of the sexes in outer space."

"The project team thought about it thoroughly, don't you think? Probably right from the start, when they selected the crew."

"Sure, they pondered it. But what could they really do?" asked Tina.

"Not much, I guess. I'm not concerned with myself as much as I am with the others. It's not that I'm a saint, or anything even close, but I'm sure I can control myself sexually for the sake of this mission, even though we're talking decades. This voyage is what has driven me for years, but I do find myself occasionally worrying about the rest of the crew, and how they will impact me."

"You know, Coug, I've thought long and hard about it, too. The project team could have solved this easily by selecting an all-male crew, but they didn't. Let's just put our faith in them. They haven't missed a beat, so far."

"There's a unique solution I've thought about," said Cougar, a curl of her lower lip providing a hint of a practical joke gone wild.

"And that is?..."

"Well, right from the beginning, I was pretty sure you were either lesbian or bisexual, since I saw you shrugging off the guys, in a captain-like manner, of course. But..."

"You know what I assumed?" interrupted Tina.

"I could guess."

"Well, your haircut and all those masculine muscles make you look like a tomboy. I mean it in an admiring sort of way."

"Sure, sure. Everyone thinks I'm a dike. I'm used to it. Which is what I'm suggesting might be to our advantage."

"Okay, sorry to interrupt. What's your idea?"

"Well, if we're both homosexual, that solves it. It's as good as an all-male crew. Problem solved."

Cougar pushed back in her chair and raised both of her thumbs, with an artificially victorious grin, waiting for Tina to absorb what she'd said. Tina tilted her head and scrunched her eyebrows in a negative posture before she replied.

"Maybe it would work. Until another few light-years from here, when someone on the crew tries to test whether it's nature or nurture."

After that evening, nothing really changed. But once in a while, just to make sure the rest of the crew got the hint, they touched their fingers together briefly when they knew others were watching. Nothing different, just more obvious.

It seemed to work. Cougar noticed that the sexual advances she'd perceived from Doctor Don seemed to suddenly disappear. She made sure she didn't push him away, since his gruff personality meant he had no one else to turn to, but he was noticeably less assertive with her.

As for Tina, she remained at ease in her friendship with Cougar, just as before, and still without a hint of overt sexuality. However, Cougar sensed a change in Tina that pulled them apart just a little, or maybe it was a change in Cougar herself. "Girlfriend" still grated a bit.

Cougar's relationship with the rest of the crew was magnificent, at least as far as she self-evaluated the situation. She'd never been a social animal, except when it came to her intense involvement in team sports back on Earth, especially soccer and basketball. She had never felt so comfortable with a group as she did this crew. But that too had changed a bit since her hibernation, especially when it came to her on-and-off confrontations with Don Mercedes.

"I suppose I'll have to keep thanking you for the next hundred light-years for my brain surgery," said Cougar after a handball session in the ship's gym, her first strenuous activity since normal gravity was restored.

The gymnasium was one of the most important rooms on the ship. Everyone spent time here both individually for a workout, one-on-one for a game of handball or hoops, or as a complete crew for beach volleyball minus the beach. The gym and dining areas were the lifeblood of the galactic crew. Both gave comfort, and both had multiple purposes. Movies and social events were conducted in either room, depending on the nature of the occasion.

When it came to sports, Cougar was generally at the top of the standings, and Don Mercedes was almost always at the bottom. But entire crew engaged in sporting activities nearly equally, for they all understood the importance of maintaining muscle tone, structural strength, coordination, and mental health. A good workout aboard the ship contributed to each of these aspects.

"Everyone else is afraid to challenge you in handball," said Doctor Mercedes, after losing badly (again) to Cougar. "But not me. I have a natural defeatist attitude."

"Tim is pretty tough," replied Cougar. "Almost beat me the other day. He's not afraid to take risks on the court. As for you, I figure you just let me win so I don't feel bad."

"Oh, sure. This little match today shows I'm one tough dude," laughed Mercedes.

"Well, I enjoy playing against you, and it's good exercise for us both. And you're not afraid of me, are you?"

"Why should I be afraid? One of these days I'm gonna' whip your little ass."

"Trying to pay me back for making you stay awake while we all hibernated?"

"No, it was just the way things had to be, so let go of it, Coug. Nothing more than another scenario built into the mission manual. They thought of everything when they put this project together, even what to do when a butch navigator needs brain surgery."

"You could have appealed to Tina," said Cougar. "She can override the flight manual with a twitch of her cute little lips. And she would, if she thought it was best for the ship. But you didn't even ask."

"Well, it's pretty well known that I'm not the Captain's favorite. In fact, in the pecking order, I don't even get to peck. Besides, I wouldn't have wanted to take the chance of putting myself into cryo-sleep. I happen to know how difficult the hibernation process is when it's not conducted in the all-crew automated format. I didn't even want to administer it to you, although I had plenty of control over the process. To try putting yourself to sleep would be like practicing self-hypnosis. You might not wake up to see the results."

"So were those five years as difficult as I imagine?" asked Cougar.

"Not really. Lots of time to catch up on my reading. As I said before, let it go."

"You know, Don, maybe you remember something about an extended period during our hibernation when the ship slowed down for some reason. We still don't have any explanation for the donut ring anomaly. I assume you checked the vitals on the bridge every day."

"Not every day, and even then only because it was something to do. Absolutely everything was automated, and we just kept plugging along straight-ahead at 0.31 SOL, day-after-day."

"No unusual pings on the meteor detector?" asked Cougar. "Nothing indicating something that might have slowed us down?"

"No, nothing. There were some pings, and I logged them, but nothing extensive. Just the typical small hits now and then. It's all in the log."

"I know. Tina has reviewed it pretty extensively. Must have been mighty boring."

"That it was," replied Mercedes.

"Unless, of course, you were maneuvering the ship around on your own, just to teach us a lesson."

"No! No, of course not," said Mercedes with a smug stare.

"Just kiddin'! Don't take me so seriously."

"That's what Tina says. She tells me to lighten up with the rest of you. To tell you the truth, except for you, I don't take anyone very seriously around here. And it's no secret how they feel about me."

"You're a critical crewmember, Don. We all know how much we need our doctor. Some just show it in funny ways. Like how Kenny is always clowning around. It's hard to tell when he's being serious and when he's just gearing up to play a joke on somebody."

"I'm not concerned about it," said Mercedes. "Because the truth of the matter is that I really don't care about them. I'm here to do a job, and that's it. So why don't you just run on home to your little girlfriend, and we'll call it a day."

Cougar twisted her head away from Mercedes, an unconscious reaction like a flinch when you suddenly remember something important. She knew Don didn't have a great bedside manner, but she didn't think there was more to it than that. She'd always assumed he was simply a bit short on personality, and made everyone pay for it.

But sometimes she wondered if there wasn't more to it than met the eye.

A crew traveling through 100 light-years of space needs a doctor. But they also need a mutual level of understanding that instills a sense of support from everyone on the crew. Cougar knew that Don Mercedes would have to change his attitude towards teamwork someday, but she wasn't sure when, and certainly not how.

## Chapter 7

## **Girlfriends**

"Have you and Mercedes been getting along okay?" asked Cougar, as she climbed into her upper bunk.

Tina sat in the rocking chair below, pajamas already on, waiting for Cougar to settle into her bed before climbing into her own lower bunk.

"As good as a captain and a ship's doctor can get along, considering his personality," replied Tina. "But who am I to say. Everybody gripes about Mercedes, but they also kid about their lesbian captain behind her back."

"Tina, that's not what I meant."

"I know, but I'm concerned about this little charade we're playing around the rest of the crew. It might solve the problem of sexual tension between guys and gals, but a mission commander shouldn't be playing games like this."

"I never thought about it that way. I just..."

"I know, Coug. I didn't mean to go off on a tangent, but I think we need to reconsider how we present ourselves to the rest of the crew. Let's give it some thought, so it's fair to everyone. Maybe we can talk about it later."

"Sure. That'd be fine. The mission is going nearly perfect, and I certainly don't want our relationship to mess things up. As long as I can still bunk with you, of course. I really enjoy that."

"Me too. Okay, now back to your original question, which really has nothing to do with this. Don Mercedes is a tough nut to crack, but his medical skills are excellent, and I can't knock anything he's done so far except how he aggravates the rest of the crew. On a long voyage like this, if it wasn't him, it'd be something else. So maybe his temperament is better to deal with than whatever might take its place. I'm fine with him."

"I agree. I've always thought his personality wouldn't be an operational problem. But he told me today he didn't care about the rest of the crew. He said it in a way that made me think he someday might do something that isn't in the best interest of the mission. And there's a lot of 'somedays' ahead of us."

"Does it seem more extreme than before our cryogenic period?"

"Yes, that's exactly the point. If he's slipping in a negative direction, then I'm concerned. But it sounds like you haven't noticed it."

"No, I haven't," replied Tina. "In fact, I thought it might head that way after he was forced to be alone for a five-year stretch, but it didn't even seem to phase him. That in itself has given me cause to wonder?"

"To wonder what?" asked Cougar.

"Well, why was he so undisturbed by what we put him through? Any normal person would have been adversely affected, but he seemed to take it in stride. Maybe he's stronger in character than he shows on the surface."

"So here's a guy we all think is completely lacking in persona, and maybe he's got more of it than any of us."

"Or maybe he really is a problem waiting to blow. I'll try to breach the subject when I talk to him next time, Coug, but you can help. You're the only one he pays any personal attention to, so give him whatever friendship you can. Maybe you can help turn him around. One thing for sure, he may not need us, but we certainly need him."

Cougar wiggled around, adjusting her sheet and blanket in the tiny space of her upper bunk, trying to accept Tina's viewpoint. As she settled into her bed, sliding her pillow up under her head, she added: "Okay, Captain. I'll work on it."

Tina stood up from the rocking chair, turned off the light, and stepped across to her own bunk bed.

"Good night, Lieutenant," said Tina.

"Good night, girlfriend," replied Cougar.

\* \* \* \* \*

W!TH THE FIRST THOMSON-JUMP behind them, most of the unknowns seemed to be resolved, and it was a relief to everyone. Their first session of cryogenic sleep was flawless, and their initial jump was textbook perfect. Of course, there was the unusual instance of brain surgery in space and a crewmember who didn't participate in the hibernation process. But the ship's systems were performing without a single fault, and the crew was healthy. Now it was just a matter of performing these same functions of cryo-sleep and Thomson-Jump two more times in sequence until reaching their destination. Then, of course, there was the matter of landing on a new planet, and eventually going home.

After the space jump, the ship was no farther off target than the error radius of the original donut, and it was mostly speed-line error, so there wasn't anything to be done about it. They couldn't go any faster, so they could only accept the anomaly and press on. The slight off-course orientation was taken care of with rocket correction pulses that had minimal impact on their fuel reserve. In another few months, they'd enter their cryogenic cubes for a fully automated hibernation for all six members of the crew.

As they approached the period of cryo-sleep, Cougar had no navigation responsibilities except to project the next post-cryo position of the spacecraft. Once the new donut appeared on her workstation display, she gazed at it for a few minutes, and then said aloud to herself: "Okay, no more smart-aleck surprises, please. Either give me exactly the same error as before or none at all."

If they came out of their sleep period within the donut ring, she'd be thrilled. If the same error was repeated, it would only mean there was an unexplained force that was at least somewhat consistent, and she'd try to be satisfied. Something different from those two results would be cause for concern.

Major Lin and Sergeant Childers were busy with their systems checks, and they found not a single flaw requiring attention. The fusion engine was operating perfectly, and everything aboard the ship was within normal parameters.

Doctor Mercedes and Sergeant Halmer spent their duty time checking and rechecking all six cryogenic cubes for electrical congruity, proper nano-drug reserves, and adequate pressure, and they found the equipment in pefect shape.

Captain Brett spent most of the final days leading up to the second cryo-session reviewing the checklists associated with winding down the ship's systems to minimum energy levels. Also, all longitudinal rotation had to be stopped, to provide their hibernating bodies a zero-gravity environment for the safest cryogenic sleep. Most of these actions wouldn't be completed until the final few hours before the sleep period began, so she had spare time on her hands, which she spent in the gym. She'd be next-to-last into her cryo-pod, followed by Doctor Mercedes.

Then the ship would be silent for five more years.

## Chapter 8

## To Sleep, Perchance to Dream

Captain Tina Brett and Dr. Donald Mercedes floated from one cryo-cube to another, making sure all biological readouts for the rest of the crew were stable before entering their own pods. At first, Tina thought Tim Halmer's pulse rate and respiration were unusual compared to the other four cubes, but Doctor Mercedes pointed out the reason.

"Nothing to worry about, Captain. He's just started dreaming, earlier than the rest. Normal vital signs for such a thing."

"Time to do it," replied Tina. "I'd prefer to be a few minutes ahead of the countdown clock."

"Wouldn't want to mess with the Princess," he said, referring to the female voice that called out the sequence of required events.

Tina laughed. Lately, Don Mercedes seemed less confrontational than normal. After her discussion with Cougar, Tina had talked to Mercedes at length, trying to get him to open up and discuss whatever was perpetually bothering him. By the end of their easy-going half-hour of conversation, she personally pronounced him almost-normal, and certainly not a threat to the mission or anyone aboard the ship. Cougar agreed – she too felt he was easier to get along with now, as if his harsh words with Cougar had given him cause to soften his personality a bit. Both Tina and Cougar were glad the potential problem seemed to be taken care of before their cryogenic session, feeling Don would be even less disruptive after five years of forced sleep.

"Cryogenic countdown – forty-two minutes," said the Princess in her sometimes-scolding tone. "All remaining crewmembers should proceed to their assigned chambers. Auto-action to begin in thirty-seven minutes."

"Tsk, tsk. Better get going," said Tina. "See you in a few years."

\* \* \* \* \*

CRYOGENIC HIBERNATION FOR SPACE travelers had been introduced over a hundred years ago, first for relatively short periods, then extending up to 12 years. However, such prolonged stretches had proven damaging to the human body. In the last few decades, the process had been limited to five-year increments, with multiple awake-sleep cycles for a lengthy voyage. This worked well for transport of the first colonists to the nearest stars. Thomson-Jump technology was still in its infancy, so these travelers endured as many as five cryogenic cycles on the way to their destinations. But repeated cycles also proved damaging to the overall human condition, which was another reason the missions were never planned as two-way voyages. Even with this much experience in cryogenic sleep, the process was so touchy that it was still considered experimental.

Today's cryo-technology incorporated several new innovations, including significant improvements to the wake-up phase, where psychotic effects associated with disorientation and amnesia previously prevailed for weeks or even months. The most significant physical effect that troubled the still-adolescent science was potential damage to chilled tissues.

Much of the recent advancement in the overall process was due to better bioengineering. Nano-medicine was now used throughout the hibernation period to provide space travelers with a steady supply of pharmaceuticals controlling the cryo-sleep cycle. Other advancements included improvements in artificial intelligence needed to actively control the sleep sequence.

Early failures in cryogenics led to development of the "Franklin Bronchial Catheter," which pretty much solved the major remaining problem of suspended animation, damage to the respiratory system. Other advancements allowed lowering human metabolism to the point where virtually no aging occurred, even during five-year cryo-sessions.

Reducing body temperatures wasn't a problem, since there was so little heat in outer space. Still, a successful passive system was delayed several decades because bioengineers initially focused on cryogenic systems that carried their own coolant materials aboard the spacecraft. Although this worked for some test flights within the solar system, on-board coolants proved to be a dead end for galactic travel, where the extra weight became the enemy of design.

Since the colony flights were one-way, and communications was generally abandoned before the missions were complete, it was difficult to get good feedback regarding the success or failure of cryogenics advancements as adapted to outer space. The most relevant data came from ships on which voyagers died during the early phase of their departure from Earth, which wasn't an uncommon situation. Colonial flights often sustained losses during unscheduled wake-ups early in the missions. Generally, these failures involved body rejuvenation problems that were considered minor to begin with, but could degenerate into complications, such as the always-present malady of "cryo-itch." Almost everyone awakening in a cryo-cube could expect dry, itchy skin, although advances in nano-tech moisture balance resulted in fewer and fewer instances. Still, itch could sometimes unexpectedly bloom into "freezer burn" that got out of control. Over time, the technology improved, and reports of burn were reduced, but it was impossible (so far) to completely eliminate it. Freezer burn was caused by cryo-sleep pharmaceuticals that became trapped in joints and muscles, and it could quickly kill. One of Doctor Mercedes' primary functions aboard *Challenger* was to promptly treat such situations during the wake-up period.

When Tina approached her cryo-pod for the second hibernation session, she looked back over her shoulder to make sure Doctor Mercedes was busy preparing himself at his cube only a few meters away. His back was turned to her, as he prepared to undress for hibernation. Before Tina climbed onto her form-fitting gel bed, she'd need to change into a thin hospital gown, since tightly-covered skin reacted badly to the cryogenic process, resulting in raw blisters, even freezer burn. With one hand clinging to the bed behind her, she floated in zero-gravity, literally peeling her clothes off and guiding them with her foot so they angled towards the basket below the bed. She gave them a final kick towards their destination, and then tapped her foot on the fast-latch lid, while simultaneously sliding into her hospital gown. Another glance towards Don Mercedes showed him with his back towards her, still dressed.

"Preparing ship for long-term stasis of all occupants," announced Princess. "Environmental systems are now minimized. Oxygen, scrubbers, directional rockets – all secured for cryo-session. Temperature declining per specifications. Everyone will be put on ice within one-five minutes."

At least Princess had a sense of humor, such as it was.

Tina floated down over her cryo-bed, feeling the soothing cool jets of air that would keep her suspended in the center of her chamber for the next five years.

\* \* \* \* \*

THE TIME PASSED IN what seemed only a few hours. When Cougar awoke, it was almost exactly the same as her first time in the cube. In other words, it was nauseating.

Once again, the first person she saw was Doctor Mercedes. She tried to focus on him, but when she did, she felt like she was spinning and had to throw up. As before, Doctor Mercedes had his old-fashioned stethoscope slung over his shoulder, and a smirk on his face.

"Good morning, Sunshine," said Mercedes with a forced smile. "Been in the freezer for long?"

"Feels like forever, or maybe just a few minutes. Hard to tell."

"Need this?" he asked, thrusting a plastic tray in front of her face.

"In a minute. Right now I don't know whether I want to puke or just kill myself."

"That would go adversely on my record, so I'd prefer you just puke."

"Everybody okay?" asked Cougar.

"Only the Captain and I are awake so far, but frankly she's not in the best of shape. More than the normal post-cryo complaints."

Cougar looked down the row of cubes. Two others were open, those belonging to Tina and Mercedes. Gravity seemed normal, the standard 0.7-G setting they experienced during their majority of time awake. Since Mercedes wasn't trained on transitioning the ship from zero-G to normal gravity, Tina must have felt good enough to take care of it. The lights were still low, with a gentle humming in the background that sounded like the ship's systems cranking back up to normal.

"What's wrong with her?" asked Cougar.

"Well, your little girlfriend seems to have a bad case of post-cryo itch that might be headed for freezer burn. So far, she's stable in that regard, but I'll need to watch her."

"I thought they had that solved, or at least minimized, these days."

"Not the itch, but freezer burn has become less common. Still happens in a few cases, so you never know. She's still in her cube, although the lid's up now."

Cougar tried to focus on the two open cubes, and now noticed Tina in hers. She was covered by a blue sheet, and there was evaporative moisture still coming from the chamber. Maybe she had talked Doctor Mercedes through the ship's spin-up process, or somehow he knew how to take care of it himself.

"Help me get up. I want to talk to her."

"In a minute, but first you should try to puke," he said, holding the tray in front of her again. "Doctor's orders."

## Chapter 9

## **Bulls-Eye**

They'd now voyaged almost 35 light-years from Earth, the farthest any space mission had ever traveled by more than a factor of three. The 33-light-year jump had been the biggest chunk, with two five-year cryo-sessions adding most of the rest. The target planet was still 66 light-years away, which meant another Thomson-Jump, followed by one more cryo-period, and then a final jump nearly to the destination star. The final approach into the stellar system would be a long decelerating fusion burn that could take two years, dependent upon how close the last Thomson-Jump brought them to their destination. It would be less than a year between the last two jumps and the remaining cryo-period, so time accumulated on the crew's bodies mostly between events, as well as leaving one solar system and entering the other.

During training, a classroom lecture by the world's most renowned living expert regarding Thomson-Jumps had explained the theory, keeping it simple and avoiding the math. To Cougar, it seemed more philosophical than scientific. When the question and answer part of the lecture began, Tina was the first to raise her hand.

"Is there any way to explain, in a manner we might understand, why a Thomson-Jump won't age our bodies?"

"Not really," said the Thomson expert. "Any other questions?" he laughed.

In fact, Thomson-Jumps weren't totally understood by anyone. They simply worked.

Cryogenics was more understandable – miraculous, but scientifically comprehensible. Cryo-sessions wouldn't significantly age the human body, which made sense since all bodily functions nearly ground to a halt, but hibernation periods were no easy technological feat. And things could go wrong. In the case of the most recent cryo-session, Tina was still confined to her quarters, spending almost all day in bed under the combined attention of Cougar and Doctor Mercedes. She was alert enough to discuss the ship's progress during this post-cryo phase, but freezer burn seemed to be setting in, and it was known to kill. Tina was far from out of the woods, but she had entered her cryo-cube in top physical shape, which improved her chances for recovery.

"Are all of the ship's systems back up to 100 percent?" she asked Cougar on the third day in her quarters, the first intelligible conversation they had been able to muster since her cryo-lid came open.

"Everything's fully operational, with no problems," replied Cougar.

"Are we in the donut?"

"As a matter of fact, we're smack-dab in the middle this time."

"I don't see a smile on your face," replied Tina, making Cougar feel a lot better to see her friend sounding almost as normal as ever.

"Well, in some ways I'm thrilled. But it makes our original off-course excursion even more mysterious."

"Meaning what?" asked Tina.

"Not now. You need to gear up slowly. Let's not steal all of your energy at one time. It's great to see you talking like this, but everything about the ship can wait. I promise I'll brief you on the details when you're stronger. For now, let's talk about other stuff."

"I don't want to talk about other things, Coug. I want to talk about my ship."

"Of course," said Cougar in a resigned voice. This was the old Tina, and she was glad to have her back.

"So tell me about the position fix," said Tina.

"Well, it was perfectly normal. Right in the bulls-eye. Since the projected course worked out perfectly this time, including the speed-line, I've been trying to figure out what was different during the first sleep period."

"For one thing, we were closer to Earth, if that makes any difference," said Tina, looking perkier the more they talked.

"True. I thought of that, but I can't see how it would affect the situation."

"So what else have you come up with?" asked Tina.

"Well, this is really grasping at straws, but there's a common thread about Mercedes."

"Mercedes. What do you mean?"

"For one thing, he was awake during our first cryo-session, for the full five years. And he was asleep in the second session."

"So what are you driving at, Coug?"

"There's another difference involving Mercedes." Cougar paused, as if she was afraid to continue. "Besides being awake when we deviated from our flight plan, he was the last person to go to sleep this time."

"Sure. But I don't see..."

"I feel like I'm being totally paranoid," said Cougar. "He's a pretty weird guy, although I admit I kinda' like him. But you ended up sick this time, and you went to sleep just before him."

"Which implies what? – That he put some arsenic in my wine or something."

"Well, he's a medical expert, and he knows a lot about cryo-cubes. It might not be arsenic in wine, but it could be almost anything in your nano-drugs."

"Oh, great. So you think we have a psychopathic deviant in our midst."

"No, no! I'm just saying the flight plan segment on the first cryo-session didn't score a bulls-eye, and my captain got sick on the second. And Mercedes was in the vicinity of the action both times."

\* \* \* \* \*

AFTER ANOTHER FEW DAYS of rest, Tina improved quickly. In the meantime, Cougar assumed her leadership duties, as was standard for a NavCom officer. Soon Tina was making occasional visits to the bridge, staying a little longer each time. Her skin was still itching, but Doctor Mercedes now proclaimed her out of harm's way as far as freezer burn was concerned. The ship returned to normal operations in all respects, with six more months at 0.13 SOL standing between the crew and their next Thomson-Jump.

During this period, there wasn't a lot to do, so the crew spent much of the time in the gym and watching movies together. Their onboard supply of Hollywood classics spanned hundreds of years, and storage space in the ship's computer was barely affected. Computer data banks had expanded enormously in recent decades, and a full movie could be compressed into less than a megabyte. So they had enough motion pictures to last a lifetime.

"Tell me a little about the nano-drugs used in our cryo-cubes," said Cougar to Sergeant Halmer one day over coffee in the dining area.

"Now what in the world brought this on?" asked Tim.

Cougar and Tim were spending quite a bit of time together lately. Tim was amazingly profound, almost an academic type, although he was a staff sergeant, the lowest rank on the ship. He brought considerable medical experience to the *Challenger* mission, having worked in cutting-edge military health facilities throughout the world. Cougar liked engaging Tim in scientific discussions, because he always was ready for a mental challenge.

"I was just wondering about the drugs used to maintain our bodies while we're in the freezer. They're similar to drugs used back on Earth, aren't they?"

"Pretty much. Doctor Mercedes and I don't have any direct contact with them, since they were all pre-programmed before we left Earth. The AI monitors everything in the cubes, though I've had some training on the administration of emergency medications in our cubes if something goes wrong. Most of the stuff is Earth-standard, nano-drugs to maintain respiration and body tone. Nothing special, really."

"If it was an emergency, how would you administer it? Through intravenous drips or what?"

"It's a lot more sophisticated than that. The whole thing is computerized through the AI, injected direct by using the nano-drug ports at the base of our cubes. Alternate drugs are already containerized and ready to go. In training, Mercedes and I used a cube simulator to practice some injections. Just pick what you want, and push the button. We have the same things in some of our bigger hospitals. We call it dial-a-drug."

"Do you have to override the AI first, or can you do it without even getting a warning from Princess?"

"Nothing to it. It's considered an emergency procedure, so you just have at it, and the AI gets out of the way. I don't think Princess would utter a peep."

"Sounds pretty simple," said Cougar.

"So why are you interested?"

"Oh, you know me. Just interested in how things operate. Could also be a good way to get some middle-of-the-night meds when I'm in the mood."

"It would be easier to just ask your friendly technohealth specialist. He's always ready to please."

\* \* \* \* \*

"NICE GAME," SAID COUGAR, still panting after a round of handball with Don Mercedes. Her sweaty short hair looked curlier than normal, with her ears sticking out in an unattractive way.

"It's nicer when you win," replied Mercedes. "Personally, I don't know what that feels like."

"It feels exhausting – that's what it feels like. Thanks for the game. Say, Doc, do you think Tina will be more at risk during our next hibernation, considering her condition this time?"

"No, she's fully recovered. Why do you ask? Isn't she good in bed these days?"

"Very funny. No, I was just wondering if there were any danger signs we need to look for."

"Danger signs? She's over it, Coug. Done. End of story."

"Well, how do you think she got so close to freezer burn? Could her cube have something wrong with it?"

"Of course not. It was just one of those things. The AI keeps close track of everything involving the drugs in the cubes. There would be an immediate error report if something went astray. Besides, there's nothing to go wrong in a cube that's backed up by at least three different subsystems."

"Did you notice anything unusual when she went to sleep?" asked Cougar, trying to act nonchalant.

"What would I notice? She said 'So long!' and we went our separate ways. Quite a body, as you know, when she slips out of those clothes."

"You didn't steal a look?" said Cougar with a credible laugh.

"No, just kidding. Look, there's nothing abnormal about her cube. Things like this just happen. Trust me, medicine isn't really a science."

"Spoken by someone who should know," replied Cougar.

## Chapter 10

## Glitch

At Cougar's workstation in the bow, the stars were blocked by the shutters that had been moved into place. With the ship rotating to produce their normal gravity, it would be somewhat disturbing to their kinesthetic senses to look out the front viewport, so they ran with the bow windows covered.

Cougar called up the canned choices on her Nav Scenarios screen, and selected "Track History." Zoomed far out, their track curved as it exited the solar system, until it steadied into a straight line headed "true north," and then ran flat and unswerving all the way to their present position, with no deviations in direction visible at this scale.

Cougar used the screen pointer to draw a rectangle around the first part of the straight section. Then she zoomed in to display a now-fatter straight line running from the bottom of the screen to the top. Touching the icon for "Chronological Labels," dates popped up adjacent to the line. Using the visible labels, she boxed the line further, until "September 23, 2235" was on the bottom, and "April 7, 2241" on top, encompassing the beginning of their direct trajectory after exiting the solar system until the end of the first five-year sleep session.

At this point in their journey, dates seemed meaningless. The crew still lived by Earth's calendar and chronometers, as a matter of convenience and to minimize the impact on their body clocks. September and April were no longer related to seasons or the position of the sun. Yet the crew celebrated the Earth's normal holidays, with imposed breaks to their work schedule and major (for them) feasts.

Tina had already surveyed the ship's automated log, looking for any anomalies in their track that might have caused their excursion outside the original donut, or any slowing of their journey through space. Although she had found nothing unusual, Cougar's automated navigational record was based on data from a different volume of the ship's computer than Tina's. There was no reason to suspect the results would be different, but Cougar had the time and the inclination, so she inspected the straight line for any variations that might be present.

To zoom in farther would allow a closer look, but five years of data would take some time to inspect. Since she had to start somewhere, she drew a box around the first few months on the bottom of the screen, representing the beginning of their hibernation period. It took her the rest of the afternoon to work through the first few days of data, literally hour-by-hour. When she headed to her quarters at the end of her scheduled shift, she had advanced only a few days beyond the date of her surgery, when both she and Doctor Mercedes were still awake (Cougar less so than Mercedes as she entered her post-op recovery period). The rest of the crew was already asleep, the course-line was running straight, and the speed-line clicked steadily along at precisely 0.130273 SOL.

To determine their track, she simply examined the line for straightness, using a digital tool that looked like a miniature old-fashioned carpenter's level. She lined it up along the line, and watched the deviation bar in the box beside it – 0.0000 all the way. For the speed line, she used a similar tool looking like a standard ruler, with a scale of a thousandth of a light-year per segment. Aligning the ruler along the track (where it immediately snapped into place), she could read out the time between hashed segments on the line. Once again, a digital display showed the ship's velocity for each segment, converted directly into distance traveled per unit of time – a displayed velocity of "0.130273 SOL" on-and-on along the line.

When Cougar returned to her workstation the next day, she continued the tedious task of analyzing each segment beyond the ninth day of crew hibernation (Cougar's third day of cryo-sleep). The line still ran straight north (meaning directly towards their destination), and the segments on the track remained perfectly spaced. Then, unexpectedly, during the third week of crew sleep, the speed-line box began flashing red.

"Whoa!" said Cougar out loud.

"What's that Nav?" said Major Lin, positioned behind her at his workstation. They were the only two on the bridge, and Kim Lin thought she must have been talking to him.

"Oh, sorry, Kim. I just don't believe what I'm seeing. It looks like we made a quick deceleration while everyone was asleep during our first cryo-session."

"No way," said Kim calmly, as if he didn't believe her. "Shoot it over to me."

Cougar touched the "Send to Engineer" icon on her screen, and the data immediately flowed to Kim's workstation. Meanwhile, she jotted a quick note on her side-slate: "0.130269 – Decel."

The course-line was still running perfectly straight, but the speed-line box flashed the sudden deceleration: "-0.000004." If the reading was correct, the ship had slowed down suddenly. She quickly scanned ahead to the next segment, and the red box remained, with the deviation even larger: "-0.000007."

"Must be a glitch," said Major Lin. "I reviewed all of the ship's system data, like Tina asked, and everything remained perfectly normal during the first hibernation period. She says the ship's automated log confirms it, too. We're looking at a nav system error. You're on a different storage volume, you know."

"Sure, I know, Kim," said Cougar quickly, wanting to get back to her screen. "But maybe that's why I'm picking up the deceleration. The Captain's log and your subsystems are on the same volume, so maybe yours is the one in error."

"I doubt it," replied Kim, as if he was sure of himself.

"Why would your volume be any more accurate than mine? More to the point, why would they differ at all?"

"Well, for one thing, the Captain's log is on my volume," replied Kim. "The designers would have assured it was the most accurate, since it's..."

"Bullshit!" interrupted Cougar. "Are you saying they constructed one volume less precise than another on purpose? That's stupid."

She immediately regretted her choice of words. Kim was one of the smartest crewmembers, with a documented IQ only slightly less than Doctor Mercedes. He was precise in all of his duties and never a problem for Cougar. But lately he seemed a bit antagonistic, especially in recent days when she saw him in the dining area. Twice she had walked in on heated discussions between Lin and Mercedes, catching a few words that seemed purposefully disrespectful of Tina.

Of course, a little natural grumbling was standard in any organization, regardless of the professional quality of the crew. And the Captain was an easy target for any discontent, no matter how minor. Cougar, being Tina's bunk-mate, was left out of most of the discussions. No one seemed sure whether she and Tina were lovers or just roommates, but it was obvious to everyone that they were sincere friends. So talk sometimes switched to a different topic when Cougar entered the room. It was probably nothing to be concerned with, certainly well short of anything that could be described as mutiny, but it left Cougar with a bad taste in her mouth. It seemed Kim Lin was as much to blame for the over-coffee talk regarding Tina as anyone else aboard the ship, even Mercedes.

"The volumes are on a priority system," replied Kim calmly. "The ship's log gets first attention, as it should."

"Of course. I know that," replied Cougar defiantly.

Sometimes Kim treated her like a child. Today he seemed to be insisting he knew more than she did, for no apparent reason, since the real issue was the data being displayed. From a scientific point of view, the focus should be on following the historic record to conclusion, rather than arguing about its validity. Disputing the data could come later.

Kim became silent, as if he was done with his argument, so sure of himself that it didn't warrant any further discussion. Which was fine with Cougar, since she wanted to return to her investigation.

When she shifted to the next time increment on her screen, the deceleration increased even further: "-0.000016."

"Shit! The velocity is dropping like a rock!" she said out loud, immediately regretting subjecting herself to Kim's analysis.

Major Lin said nothing, which Cougar took to mean he was completely ignoring her and the data now displayed on both of their screens.

Moving another segment forward, Cougar was appalled at what she saw. The flashing red box read "-0.000083" and the image was now accompanied by the course-line box that was also flashing. The track changed from "0.0000" to "-0.0001." The ship was deviating to the left as well as continuing to rapidly decelerate.

If this maneuver was real, it indicated either a major systems malfunction or an automated action to avoid something. Maybe a chunk of unexpected space-rock had suddenly appeared in front of the ship, although the AI was generally able to see far enough ahead to avoid course or speed changes visible on any scale Cougar would be able to investigate. Yet here it was – their ship was suddenly decelerating and now veering to the left.

Cougar quickly scanned ahead, one frame after the other, watching the speed decrease further, while the track changed by only a small amount, the equivalent of less than five degrees, until the speed box changed to steady red with the number inside now blinking: "-0.130269 * * FWD VEL 0.000004."

Their ship was all but stopped.

Cougar was exhausted by the implications. Her heart pounded in her chest, and her respiration went up. She felt beads of sweat on her forehead. Meanwhile, Kim sat silent behind her, either ignoring all he saw or simply deciding not to comment on it.

She scanned forward a few more segments, and the numbers blinked at her, unchanging. The track was now nearly constant at 355.0708 relative to true north, slowly drifting fractions of a degree to the left, and the ship was steady at a speed equating to only a few thousand kilometers per hour.

This couldn't be real. If it was, their bodies would have experienced a tremendous shock during the extreme deceleration, and certainly that would have appeared readily on the ship's log and the system readouts.

Then again, it totally concurred with the donut anomaly displayed after their first cryo-session. They had slipped well behind on the speed-line and slightly to the port side of their intended track. Logic said such a sudden stop without being highlighted on the ship's log would be impossible. The facts said otherwise.

*****

TINA WAS ON THE mountain-climb simulator in the gym when Cougar summoned her to the bridge. She walked the short distance immediately, still wearing her shorts, T-shirt, and visor cap, and sweating rather profusely from her climbing exercise. She was breathing hard, and her rose-tinted lips puffed out even more lusciously than normal.

Major Lin called out the routine acknowledgment: "The Captain is on the bridge."

"At ease, everyone," replied Tina, acknowledging the standard greeting.

She slid into her seat on the raised platform behind the other workstations, noticing Kim Lin was pushed back in his seat, reading something from the data on his side-slate. Cougar was hunched over her screen, busy at whatever she was doing, undoubtedly expecting the "at ease" command and not missing a beat.

"Hello, Captain," said Cougar as calmly as possible. "Got something for you to look at."

Tina was already entering her password, and her computer display was booting up.

"Send it," replied Tina.

Almost before Tina finished her clipped statement, her screen filled with the relayed display from Cougar's station.

"Holy shit! When was this?" she exclaimed.

"That's what I said," laughed Cougar, breaking her own self-imposed concentration for the first time in the last hour. "This screen shot is during Day 34 of our first cryo-period. The deceleration began nine days earlier, and progressed all the way down to almost zero in that short span. The off-course deviation began five days after the deceleration started, and now shows a slow drift to the left while nearly stopped."

"No way!" said Tina. "The ship's log doesn't even show any deviations, and Kim's systems report didn't indicate any abnormalities either."

"But this plot shows otherwise. It shows a rapid deceleration, then almost stopped and drifting slightly to the left, backing up what we saw on the original donut error. I've been scanning further ahead for the last few minutes, and we remained nearly stopped for three days, then slowly accelerated back up to speed. It would explain the donut error almost exactly."

"So how do we account for the difference between this data and the lack of deviation on the ship's log or the systems analysis? Even if my log was farbled for some reason, Kim's parameters shouldn't have been affected. I mean, how could we go through a severe deceleration like this without showing up on the fusion thrust plot or all of the ship's subsystems?"

"You and Kim are on a different storage volume than me," replied Cougar. "So maybe one of the volumes is in error."

"I don't see how it could make a difference. Weren't the volumes built to exactly the same specs?"

"That's what I thought, but Kim says the ship's log was constructed to a higher standard."

When Cougar turned around to suggest to Kim that he provide his inputs, the seat behind her was already empty.

\* \* \* \* \*

"So give me some ideas, Coug," said Tina once they were back in their quarters, Cougar already in her pajamas, and Tina still in her mountain climbing garb.

"It's pretty amazing, isn't it?" replied Cougar. "Maybe the most surprising part isn't the results on my computer, but the difference between our two volumes. How could that have occurred?"

"Computers do go berserk," suggested Tina. "Don't forget – they're all quantum computers."

"True. But such a big difference. According to my data, the deceleration and subsequent re-acceleration extended over a period of several weeks. Certainly it should have been detected on your computer as well as Kim's, or some kind of an error message should have been displayed. If it had been just your log or just Kim's data, I might buy into the idea of some kind of glitch in the computer or its software. But to find no velocity deviations in either of your logs seems extremely improbable. More likely my plot is in error."

"But it agrees with the donut," countered Tina.

"Yes, it does. I keep coming back to that, too. But Kim seems totally convinced it's my data that's messed up."

"And you believe him, all things considered?" asked Tina, with a hint of suspicion tainting her question.

"Well, I'll admit I don't like his attitude of late, but I'm sure he knows more about these things than we do. Unless, of course..."

"Go on...," prompted Tina.

"Well, I hate to say it. But... unless, for some reason, he's purposely lying."

◊ ◊ ◊ ◊ ◊ ◊

## Chapter 11

## Noodles

COUGAR SPENT THE NEXT few days reviewing the plotted navigational data in more detail. She broke the chronological segments into day-to-day and then hour-to-hour chunks, applying her arsenal of navigational tools to the deceleration. She called up computer simulations in the Nav Scenarios menu, providing a three-dimensional glimpse of the movement of the spaceship, and used the navigational "noodle" to help her understand the path of *Challenger* as it rapidly slowed and started drifting to the left.

The noodle was normally employed only in real time to project the track of the ship when maneuvering in tight situations, like docking or entering a preplanned orbit. The thin extension line on the current track projected where the spacecraft would be a few minutes or hours in the future. When they entered a holding pattern in preparation for docking (which, so far, she'd experienced only in simulator training), the noodle bent in an arc that depicted where the spaceship would be in the immediate-future, dependent on all the variables of maneuvering, such as deceleration, course correction thrusters, and flight control inputs. In the case of the historic data, she could take a route segment and watch the noodle respond as *Challenger* slowly ground to a near-stop, and then watch the ship drift for days before the noodle began to grow again during acceleration.

"Run that last segment for me one more time, Coug" said Tina, after reviewing the deceleration sequence. "I wonder why the ship slowed so close to dead in the water, but never came to a complete stop."

Cougar ran the sequence again, until it finally terminated with the ship's forward velocity only 0.000004 SOL, the noodle now angled off to the left. The thin projection line shortened to almost nothing, and then tilted more to the port side as the spaceship began drifting in that direction.

"Extremely slow, but not stopped," said Cougar. "Can't think of any reason why that would occur, even if it was on purpose, unless a ship-to-ship transfer was about to occur. You wouldn't need to come to a complete stop to manage a docking and boarding operation."

"Docking with who?" asked Tina.

Kim, seated in front of Tina, turned around in his chair, as if he was about to interrupt. Then he apparently thought better of it, and returned to his screen, which was showing the same display.

"You have an idea, Kim?" asked Tina.

"No, ma'am. Nothing really."

"Coug, is there any way to determine if there were any other vessels in our vicinity when the deceleration occurred."

"Not using any of my nav gear. But there might be something built into our onboard surveillance equipment that I don't know about."

"No, I would have been briefed on such a system. Unless... Kim, is there anything in your systems tools like that?"

"Nothing, Captain. I guess the project team didn't figure they needed to protect us from ourselves. Who else would be out here?"

"Pirates, maybe," chimed in Doctor Mercedes from his workstation next to Kim, his screen idle and blank with a cursor blinking, while he read something on a hand-held notepad.

"If so, they'd probably be disgruntled colonists from Earth," joked Cougar. "Who knows what became of them all."

"Bless them if they were able to muster the technology to become space travelers again," said Tina, sounding like she felt sorry for them. "After what they must have gone through to establish themselves on those god-forsaken worlds, I wouldn't expect any of their second or third generation offspring to be alive."

It was a sober thought, and no one chose to respond to Tina's comments, so she spoke again: "Any other ideas? Serious ones, that is."

Sergeants Halmer and Childers were at the table behind her, listening in on this impromptu all-crew meeting. Tina turned towards them, and lifted her head in an obvious invitation to join in.

"Nothing, Captain Brett," said Tim Halmer.

"Not sure why the systems data didn't show anything," offered Kenny Childers. "We track a ton of parameters to make sure all of the ship's components are operating within limits. Such a quick deceleration would have pushed pressures and temperatures off the chart. But not a single warning was recorded."

"Did you review the record yourself, Kenny?" asked Tina.

"No, Captain, but Major Lin looked at all of the data strips, and nothing unusual turned up."

"Kim, would it help to have Kenny look over those strips again," asked Tina. "He might see something you missed."

When Kim swung around, his face was red, like he was mad at his sergeant for speaking out on the matter. But his facial tension eased as he spoke.

"There's nothing to see. Every subsystem parameter was flat as a pancake. It's not like Cougar's data, which can be broken into smaller segments for increased detail. The system readouts are really only warning thresholds. As long as everything stays within limits, the data flat-lines. An error signal would stand out so obvious that it couldn't be ignored."

"True, Captain," said Kenny, as if he was trying to get back on Kim's good side. "I've seen error markers like those – you can't miss them."

"Okay, so it's a dead end," noted Tina. "There's no record of anything going astray within our ship systems, my log data shows no conformity breaks of any type, and we have no surveillance data to give us a clue about anything going on inside or outside the ship. But Cougar's nav noodle is wavering all over the place, telling us something substantial happened. We'll resolve this somehow, so everybody needs to keep working on ideas, no matter how far out they may seem. For example, we may have no recorded data except Cougar's, but we did have an on-the-spot observer. Don, are you sure you don't remember anything special about what happened during those two months?"

"Like I've told you before, Captain, there was nothing unusual, except for my settling in after Cougar's brain surgery. Everything was particularly quiet with everyone but me asleep. The ship was well established and stable, as it is during a sleep period. No deceleration, no pirates, nothing at all unusual."

"And the medical archived data for the cryo-pods shows nothing?" asked Tina.

"All is normal there, too. Any rapid maneuvering of the ship would turn up as changes in our vital signs during cryo-sleep. The human body simply can't experience such extreme forces, even during hibernation, without showing some changes in pulse rates, respiration, blood pressure. But not one of you registered even a small variation in your vital signs. There simply couldn't have been the acute maneuvering Cougar found in her nav plots."

"No, Don, there's no argument about what I found," replied Cougar, a bit defensively. "The only dispute is why my data differs from Tina's and Kim's."

"Okay, okay, Cougar," said Don Mercedes in a tone indicating he wanted to move on to something else. "Your data was perfect, just like you are. Just ask Captain Brett."

"Don, that's enough!" said Tina. "The last thing we should be doing now is bickering among ourselves. We need to work together to come up with some ideas. Now listen up, everyone – We won't dismiss this as just one of those things. Even if it's an error in Cougar's data, we need to find out why it happened. There could be an underlying systems failure about to occur, and we're 35 light-years from home. In one more Thomson-Jump, we'll be well past the point-of-no-return, so there'll be no turning back. Unless some of you want to risk ignoring this and possibly jeopardizing our mission and our lives, it's time to pull together. I want everyone to devote the next few days to reviewing their assigned data for the first sleep period. Look at everything all over again. Peek in every nook and cranny for hints that might show any abnormalities. And keep your minds open to anything and everything. In fact, I'll start the list of possibilities right now, and here it is."

Tina began to write longhand on her side-tablet with a light pen, and the list appeared simultaneously on all of their tablets. She read them off one-by-one as she wrote:

"Number 1 – Systemic failure of the nav plot data," said Tina. She paused momentarily, and then continued. "Number 2 – Fusion drive glitch causing a quick deceleration and then correcting itself."

"Number 3… Let's have some more ideas right now," she prompted.

"Pirates," said Tim Halmer.

Everyone laughed, but Tina stopped them in their tracks.

"Okay, why not? Number 3 – Pirates, maybe disgruntled colonists."

"Anything else for now?" asked Tina, when the bridge fell silent.

"If we're going to include human factors, why not add the obvious?" added Cougar, her words spoken slowly, as if regretfully. "How about conspiracy."

No one moved or made a sound, waiting for Tina's reaction.

"Okay, that's Number 4 and Number 5."

She wrote the next two lines on her screen with the light pen, while simultaneously reading them out loud.

"Number 4 – Intervention of an outside intelligent source, for reasons unknown. And Number 5 – Somebody inside the ship is lying."

\* \* \* \* \*

That evening, as Cougar stepped into the gymnasium for the scheduled movie, Don Mercedes and Kim Lin were huddled in chairs side-by-side, engrossed in a heated discussion. Unlike recent days, when she entered, they seemed oblivious to her presence, and just kept talking.

"Tina doesn't trust us," said Mercedes. "If she did, she would have kept it off the list. Sure, it's obvious that conspiracy has to be considered, but what right does she have to rub it in our face."

"She sure cut you off when you questioned Cougar's data," said Kim. "Oh, Coug, I didn't see you there."

"Sure, sure. I just snuck in, and you didn't see me. Very funny."

"Well, you must admit the Captain is getting mighty demanding lately," replied Kim. "Or haven't you noticed."

"As a matter of fact, I haven't noticed. I suppose you should be running the ship."

"I don't want to run the ship," said Kim. "But I'd like it if everyone got a little more respect. Of course, when you speak, she sure listens. I wonder why?"

"Maybe because I'm making more sense lately than you two," said Cougar, her emotions suddenly elevated, feeling defensive.

"Are you making more sense to the Captain because you bunk with her, or maybe because what you have to offer is exactly the opposite of what the rest of us see," said Kim, red in the face, temper rising. "As far as I can tell, our fearless leader takes anything you say to heart. Literally."

Before Cougar answered, she tried to calm herself down. She was outnumbered, and she knew both sides of the argument were childish. Just then, Kenny walked in to interrupt their verbal sparing.

"Hi, gang!" he said in his typical less-than-serious demeanor. "I hope there ain't any of those conspirators in here tonight."

"Not in our gym," laughed Mercedes. "Super Bitch isn't here yet. Just her butch girlfriend."

"Wait a minute, Don!" said Cougar with staunchness. "Did I actually hear you call our Captain a bitch?"

"You heard it right," replied Mercedes. "Of course, I'm not the expert here. How about you? You should know."

"Don..." Cougar started to respond, and then thought better of it. Things would only get worse.

How had this deteriorated so fast? In only a few days, it seemed their situation had tumbled from a high in teamwork to a mutinous attitude making no sense. Nobody had done anything wrong, except maybe in the way they'd expressed themselves. But there was tension everywhere, and crewmembers were calling their Captain a bitch.

Time seemed to stand still as the three men in the room waited for Cougar to respond to Don Mercedes' challenge. Instead, she reflected on when this had all started. She couldn't put her finger on the exact day, but she remembered everything seemed fine earlier in the voyage, at least until after the first cryo-session. They only had a few weeks together after the hibernation and before the first Thomson-Jump, and then a few months longer before their next sleep period. So, really, it was all very recent as far as their hours awake were concerned, although the distance they had come in that brief period was nearly 35 light-years.

"So, no answer for a change," said Mercedes.

"Sorry, Don," said Cougar. "I guess everybody is a little tense these days, eh?"

* * * * *

THE MOVIE BEGAN AS soon as Tim and Tina joined them a few minutes later. They joked and hooted as they always did when the film's logo appeared on the screen. When the lion roared, Kenny Childers mocked it with his typical buffoon-like growl. Everybody laughed, and the confrontation from a few minutes earlier seemed forgotten.

The two sergeants and Kim Lin left before the movie was half over. No one seemed very interested in the docu-drama covering a famous time in history when the United States was a powerful world leader and only two political parties dominated the country's landscape. The period used as the story's backdrop was called "Watergate," which Cougar remembered studying briefly in a University of North America political science class. Her UNA poly sci professor felt the presidential era of Richard Milhous Nixon was the low point in American politics, and an important period for students to understand.

Cougar remembered that the hearings resulted in the downfall of President Nixon, but she didn't recall the details, which the movie's storyline highlighted. She watched the gym's full-wall screen as it displayed actual videotape from one of the televised Watergate sessions. The Deputy Assistant to President Nixon, Alexander Butterfield, stepped to the witness table among a background of coughs and bored rustling from the Senate committee members.

Cougar looked over at Tina, lounging curled up and half-awake in the cushy chair beside her. Don Mercedes got up to leave: "Goodnight," he said quietly. "I can't stick around to find out how history turns out."

Cougar laughed, and nodded goodbye to Don. Tina smiled at him, and said a simple "Goodnight."

In the next few minutes within the darkened gym, Lieutenant Cougar Jensen quite unexpectedly came up with an idea that shocked her and made her smile at the same time.

## Chapter 12

## Nixon's Tapes

ALEXANDER BUTTERFIELD WAS A minor celebrity in Washington when the Watergate committee sessions were televised to the nation day-after-day. Later he would go on to some fame as the Administrator of the FAA. But during his days as Deputy Assistant to the President, he became one of many routine witnesses questioned at the Senate hearings. During the proceedings, he made a simple statement that stunned the public.

Cougar watched the wall-screen with minimal interest as Butterfield was sworn in and then questioned by Republican legal counsel, Donald Sanders. Cougar remembered the Grand Old Party that had weathered so many storms before it finally disappeared from the political scene in the late Twenty-First Century. She remembered Watergate, and she knew it's what led to the downfall of Richard Nixon, but she couldn't recall most of the details, nor did she remember the name Alexander Butterfield.

Counsel Donald Sanders led off the questioning by asking Mr. Butterfield to describe his position as Deputy Assistant to the President. Butterfield's answers seemed of no interest to the committee members, who were shuffling papers and gazing in various directions. Meanwhile, Sanders asked his standard questions regarding what Butterfield thought Nixon knew about Watergate and when he knew it. When Butterfield gave his opinion, no one in the live or TV audience paid particular attention, until Sanders asked how Butterfield was so sure of Nixon's response to the Watergate burglary.

"Everything was taped," he said. "Every meeting of the President. Everything."

The coughing quieted. The committee members looked up from their notes and pulled back from their lazy gazes around the room. The stunned counsel barely knew what to say, but he said it anyway.

"Everything was taped? You mean every meeting of the president? Every phone call?"

"Everything," replied Butterfield nonchalantly.

From that moment forward, according to the docu-drama projected on the wall of the gymnasium, the situation was vastly simplified. Unknown to the public and the Senate Committee, a credible historic record was standing by to verify facts previously hidden from citizens of the most powerful nation on Earth.

"Wake up, Tina," said Cougar, as the film's credits started rolling down the wall and the gym lights came on one row at a time. "Did you see that?"

"I saw it. But if you want to know the truth, I really wasn't impressed. I mean, I get the point, but to make it into a plot that keeps your interest is a bit of a stretch. Nixon was an amazing story, but I'm not sure it comes off very well on the screen."

She was right, of course. *Challenger* had a storehouse of movies of all types. They'd seen worse, and they'd seen better. This was on the "somewhat worse" list, unless you were an avid historian. Cougar, on the other hand, saw it differently.

"But do you get the real point?" asked Cougar. "Nobody was getting anywhere with Watergate, and then suddenly this Butterfield guy comes up with a bombshell – it's all been recorded, and the mystery is going to be solved. Nobody thought the president might be taping everything for the historic record. If it was good enough for Nixon, maybe it's good enough for us."

"Meaning what?" asked Tina. "You think we've got a taped history hidden somewhere?"

"Well, why not? Wouldn't the project team provide it in case we needed it? I doubt it's hidden, but it might be tucked inside the depths of our flight manual somewhere. I remember Kim saying there wasn't such a surveillance system, but maybe he just doesn't know about it."

"Or isn't telling us," suggested Tina.

* * * * *

"There isn't such a system," said Major Lin.

"Are you sure," asked Tina. "Maybe it's something the project team built in for security or even to resolve problems like this, but didn't highlight in our training. It would have been simple to install a surveillance system in all our crew areas, the fusion compartment, too."

"I looked into it before, and there's no such equipment. No cameras anywhere, except the ones we personally use to document things and the forward-looking visual amplifier used for close-in maneuvering. Heck, do you see any camera equipment in this room, or anywhere, in fact?"

Kim sounded sure of himself, and he was the resident systems expert. Besides, as Captain, Tina would have been told about surveillance cameras, since she was ultimately in charge of all contingencies, and why else would cameras be installed except to provide security for her ship? Anything involving safety and security was in her sphere of responsibility, so she would have been briefed. Unless, of course, it was such a minor item that no one had thought to tell her, which certainly didn't sound like the ultra-thorough project team.

"Okay, Kim. But cameras are built right into other hardware these days. Look at all that stuff in the ceiling – sprinklers and sensors of all sorts. Who knows what's in the walls. Please take another look at your systems manuals, just to be sure. If you come up with a surveillance system of any kind, let me know. Even if it doesn't seem to be an aid to security, consider it of interest to our investigation."

"Investigation? Who's investigating what, Captain?"

Tina wasn't sure how to respond. Was Kim challenging her, or was it just his way of clarifying in his own mind what she was asking of him?

"You know what I'm referring to," she said as politely as she could, considering the frustration he was suddenly expressing. "Just our own internal investigation of what might have happened during the time of the deceleration."

"Alleged deceleration," replied Kim obstinately.

"Okay, alleged deceleration. Still, we need to look at it closely in case it's an indicator that one of our subsystems is about to fail."

"All of the ship's subsystems are functioning perfectly," stated Kim confidently.

"I know it appears that way to you. But maybe it's something that can't be picked up by our test equipment."

"Our test equipment is operating without any flaws, too."

Tina wasn't used to her crew responding so defensively to every little thing. But that's exactly how it seemed to be lately. The word "conspiracy" passed through her thoughts, and it didn't involve pirates.

* * * * *

"Boss, I HATE TO bring this up, but we need to talk," said Cougar, as she reclined on her upper bunk, watching Tina brush her soft blond hair in long strokes that seemed to make it lie even straighter against her cheeks.

"Uh-oh, don't tell me you're turning into a lesbian, and looking for love."

"Don't you wish?" laughed Cougar.

"I can hope, can't I?" mocked Tina.

"No, boss, this is a bit heavier than that. As I'm sure you've noticed, this crew ain't so happy these days."

"No shit! How would I have ever guessed? You don't think I see it?"

"I'm sure you see it, but probably not as clearly as I do. You're the mighty Captain, so what's said is mostly behind your back."

"That's always the way it is. So there's some news here?"

"It isn't really news," said Cougar. "It's just that it's become more noticeable. And it's happened pretty fast. Not me, of course. I'm mighty happy – your little bunk-buddy lover, you know." Cougar laughed, and then continued: "Not Tim Halmer either, and I'm not sure about Kenny Childers. But Mercedes and Lin make a dangerous pair. They're beginning to sound alike."

"Well, they are roommates, and it stands to reason that they hang out together. So just what are they saying, my little spy in the bush."

"More like a tattle-tale," replied Cougar. "And I don't like that feeling. But what they're saying is outright disrespectful, probably trying to get my goat. But there's more to it."

"Like what?" asked Tina, now done with her hair and collapsed into a pile of curled legs and arms in the soft chair.

"Well, it almost seems they're working towards something not even related to the ship's deceleration mystery. They keep bringing up how much they feel you're dictating rather than leading, and it seems like they're targeting their talk towards Halmer and Childers, maybe me, too. Trying to influence our thinking."

"Has it worked?"

"Not at all. Not just for me either. Tim Halmer is holding the line, like a crewmember should. Of course, that sits poorly with Mercedes, since Tim is under his direct supervision. It puts Tim in a hell of a spot, but he doesn't give in a bit. You'd be proud of him."

"I'm proud of the entire crew, and that includes Mercedes and Lin. But they're challenging me more than is comfortable lately. Not that I'm not used to it. It happens a little bit on any mission, but usually it's just healthy grumblings – part of the military style of doing business. But I'll admit this time, just like you, I sense something more."

"It started right after our first cryo-session," stated Cougar.

"So I noticed. Of course, that's after the deceleration occurred, if it ever did happen, that is."

"But you believe it happened?"

"I'm sure of it, Coug. And it's not just because you're my bunk-buddy lover."

\* \* \* \* \*

IT DIDN'T TAKE TINA long to find what she was looking for in the flight manual. An electronic search using the key words "Surveillance" took her right to the page. Just as Cougar had suspected, there was an elaborate imaging system installed in *Challenger*, with cameras taking pictures every few seconds in nearly all parts of the ship, including the bridge, dining area, gymnasium, and fusion compartment. The bunk spaces and bathrooms were not included in the camera coverage, a tribute to the privacy concerns of the project team. Each area had at least two cameras, with images captured at 10-second intervals for events extending back two years, making display of the time-lapse photos like viewing a jerky video. Beyond two years, the footage was stored with four-of-every-five images deleted to conserve computer storage space, producing an even bouncier video showing a frame every 50 seconds. It reminded Tina of old-fashioned convenience store security cameras, except the data covered multiple rooms, and was stored in years of files.

Either Major Kim Lin wasn't able to find the flight manual reference, or he was simply lying. Considering Tina's ease in locating the information regarding the surveillance cameras, the word "conspiracy" moved to the top of her list.

## Chapter 13

## Poseidon

WHILE HINTS OF CONSPIRACY or even mutiny passed through the thoughts of Tina and Cougar, *Challenger* approached the second of three Thomson-Jumps in their voyage to the target planet. Poseidon, formally designated 137 Herculis, had been discovered over 200 years ago, one of the first Earth-sized objects detected in the habitable zone of another solar system. In 2024, an Earth-orbiting telescope discovered a planetary system much like our own, including two Jupiter-sized objects and a watery world slightly larger than Earth. During this initial period of "sniffer" telescopes designed to detect chemical components on a scale far beyond the resolution of spectroscopes, planet searchers identified the molecules needed for life as it was known on Earth – water, carbon, and oxygen atoms bonded in sets of two. In the first year of sniffers in space, poised well above the intervening atmosphere of Earth, seventeen Earth-like planets with "intelligent-capable atmospheres" were identified within 200 light-years of our sun. In another few years, seven of these planets revealed a surface mix of liquid water and continental rock similar to Earth's.

Although the research tools progressed by leaps and bounds, the ability to positively identify intelligent life remained rudimentary. Scientists could conclusively say conditions for life existed on a specific planet, but the discovery of animal life elsewhere in the universe remained elusive. The original destinations for colonists clearly displayed the chlorophyll identifier pointing to plant life, and one initially-successful human voyage to one of the nearest stars radioed back the discovery of lush forests. Communication with this colonial mission ceased soon after its original we-have-landed report.

Poseidon become the best target-of-opportunity for the developing *Challenger* program. Although worlds with at least as much potential existed farther out in space, the biggest space mission since the *Apollo* moon-landing era was still limited in its reach. Consequently, 137 Herculis won out because of its closeness to Earth, a mere 101 light-years away, so it became the uncontested destination of the grandest technological program in history. In inflation-adjusted Gaia-dollars, *Apollo* multiple-spacecraft expenditures were less than a tenth the cost of the single *Challenger* spaceship.

With *Challenger* now 35 light-years from Earth and approaching its second Thomson-Jump, they would in an instant pass beyond the point-of-no-return. Today they were one-third of the way to Poseidon. But in another few weeks they'd be 68 light-years from Earth and two-thirds of the way to a new world with relatively unknown surface conditions.

If this mission had deteriorated so far that an aborted return to Earth was necessary, that decision would need to be made in the next few weeks. On the other hand, if they used the point-of-no-return as their guide, the most expensive technological program in history might quickly be scrapped in a tradeoff for six saved lives returned to Earth. Probably similar thoughts had gone through the minds of the original space colonists. Either human heroism or old-fashioned ego led to the multitude of must-get-there disasters that seemed to plague every mission to the stars.

"Not much chance Kim misunderstood what we were looking for," said Tina, as Cougar reached forward to trim her roommate's silky-straight hair with a pair of sharp scissors.

"Eh?"

"Well, do you see any way Kim could have missed finding the surveillance cameras? Or is it possible his database didn't have the information?"

"No way," replied Cougar, gently rubbing her thin fingers against Tina's cheek while aligning the scissors to precisely trim her soft-and-straight blond hair. "He's the system's guy. And don't forget, your volume and his are the same. He should have found the cameras right away."

"Still, it's something the project team didn't brief us about during training."

"They probably didn't feel we'd ever need the a system, but built it in just in case. I bet there's lots of stuff like that hidden in our flight manuals. Part of the reason for a human crew is to provide the flexibility needed in situations like this. Why burden our minds with things we can easily figure out ourselves when we need to?"

"Your fingers are so soft." Tina breathed the words sensuously, obviously enjoying the gentleness of Cougar's touch.

They had eliminated the sexual games they'd been playing in public, but no one knew how to interpret their bunk-mate situation. Even Tina and Cougar themselves seemed pleasantly bewildered by their enjoyable platonic relationship, occasionally punctuated by sensitive touches like this.

"So how do we handle the news about the cameras?" asked Cougar. "I mean, do you plan to let everyone know?"

"I'd normally prefer it that way. So far, I've remained pretty open with the crew about everything. But this time I think I need to be careful until we've had a chance to digest what the cameras tell us. Maybe there's nothing to see except endless hours of boredom, so let's not jump to conclusions. Then, if we find nothing to get excited about, we can release the news as if the surveillance system has just been discovered."

"Makes sense," replied Cougar. "But it's not 'endless hours' of images – it's more than 10 years worth, so it'll take a lot of time to review. The cameras will show everything since launch, including both sessions of hibernation. I guess it'll show just a quick hop through our Thomson-Jump of 33 light-years."

"But we do have a specific place to begin, where we know something unusual happened – the deceleration period early in the first cryo-session."

"And it will allow us to compare things to the nothing-happened scenario that Mercedes reports," noted Cougar.

"Yes, and I think we both know what we might find. Kim is trying to cover up something, and Mercedes is telling us he never witnessed a deceleration period while the rest of us were sleeping. We've got two troublesome personalities aboard."

"Don't you mean at least two?" asked Cougar.

\* \* \* \* \*

"Don, I apologize for asking you to go over this again," said Tina. "But we need to figure out if this deceleration occurred or not."

Dr. Donald Mercedes sat at the dining table, looking across at Tina, with Cougar next to Mercedes, leaning back in her chair.

"As I've told you before, nothing happened. There was no deceleration, and I can verify it, since I was awake when it supposedly happened. Per flight manual standards, I monitored the ship's systems during the entire period, and the so-called deceleration took nine days. Nothing happened during that period." He paused, and then began again with a more hostile tone: "Look,..." he said, pausing, then stopping.

In Cougar's mind, she heard Mercedes checking his anger in a way that indicated he wanted to say: "Look, bitch,..."

"Go ahead," said Tina.

"Well, there really isn't anything else to say. Facts are facts. End of report."

"Is there anything at all that you remember relative to unusual conditions during the first cryo-period, either before or after Cougar's brain surgery?"

"Well, I notice she's here again today, just as expected – to confirm the facts, I suppose." He nodded towards Cougar, who remained slightly pushed back in her chair, a neutral look on her face.

"Cougar is here to assist me in investigating the facts," replied Tina, sounding at her limit.

"The facts through the eyes of Cougar, your little bunk-mate."

"Enough, Don! If you come up with something helpful from the first hibernation period, be sure to let me know. In the meantime, I'll expect you to conduct yourself in a way that demonstrates complete support of this mission, including how you interact with the rest of our crew."

"And what does that mean?"

"It means I won't put up with any derogatory talk from you or anyone else on this ship that hints at insubordination."

"If anyone on *Challenger* is defying authority, I'd suggest you look closer to home. Maybe you should think about that when you go to bed tonight."

\* \* \* \* \*

"Both hibernation sessions are worth looking into," said Tina to Cougar that evening in their quarters. "We need to see what we can find during the first sleep period, of course, and whatever involvement Don Mercedes might have with the deceleration. But the second cryo-session was when I was nearly done in by freezer burn. Mercedes put me to sleep that time, which certainly makes me wonder how long he's been involved in whatever is going on."

"Lin is suspect, too," noted Cougar. "Just the existence of the cameras is enough to convince me he may be lying about other things. Maybe Mercedes and Lin are acting independently for whatever personal reasons they might have, but it's worth considering it's a conspiracy involving two or more crewmembers."

"What I don't get is what they're after," replied Tina. "The project team's screening of this crew was mighty thorough, and now all of a sudden we have at least two bad eggs telling lies for reasons that certainly aren't clear. It's not your normal mutinous behavior, considering how well the mission seemed to be going."

"You know, I've always wondered why the mission involves cryogenic sleep in the first place," said Cougar. "The distance we travel when we're in the freezer is hardly anything compared to our Thomson-Jumps, so why do we really need them? Except, of course, to save us a few years of aging. It's hard to believe it's important enough to increase the complexity of our ship so much."

"Don't forget, the Thomson-Jumps require extreme stability within the ship prior to an instantaneous hop of 33 light-years," said Tina. "Five years of crew sleep with the environmental systems nearly turned off is a good way to stabilize all of the ship's systems. Plus, there aren't any pesky humans to mess with the controls."

"I know that's what they said in training," said Cougar. "But it seems like overkill, considering the complexities that cryogenics add to the mission. Case in point — two sleep sessions and two unexplained situations, in contrast to an otherwise flawless mission that already includes one major Thomson-Jump."

"We'll know more after looking at the records from the cameras," noted Tina.

"Where do we start?" asked Cougar.

"I'll take the deceleration period, since it involves you in an unusual way," replied Tina. "Not everybody goes through brain surgery on an intergalactic spaceship, so maybe you shouldn't be the one to review that sleep session. Meanwhile, you can look into the second cryo-session to see if you can find anything pointing to freezer burn for your illustrious Captain. When you review the pictures, be careful who's looking over your shoulders."

"Let's see now," said Cougar. "Over my left shoulder sits Don Mercedes, and over my right is Kim Lin. Now there's an encouraging combination."

\* \* \* \* \*

NEITHER MERCEDES NOR LIN was on the bridge the next morning when Tina and Cougar began their camera reviews. Kenny Childers occupied Kim Lin's workstation, working on some kind of assignment from Major Lin. He seemed thoroughly occupied and not paying any attention to the work the two women were conducting at their stations. At the conference table behind them, Tim Halmer seemed engrossed in a computer game on one of the consoles. He was officially off-duty, but Tina never cared when her crew played games, even during their formal duty hours. As long as their jobs were completed efficiently, she felt no need to enforce a strict work environment. After all, they would all contribute at least half of their adult lives to this mission, and they were unofficially on-duty nearly 24 – 7.

Tina selected the two cryogenics room cameras, and displayed them split-screen on her workstation display. One of the cameras was high on the rear wall, facing towards the front of the ship, with an excellent view of the closest cryo-pods, but less detail at the other end of the room. Doctor Mercedes' cube was nearest to the camera, and her own pod was next in line. The real-time image showed today's current status, with the lids up on all cryo-cubes, which was the normal configuration between hibernation periods.

The overhead view was centered halfway between the cubes of Tim Halmer and Kim Lin, with the others off to each side. This view gave more detail for the chambers used by Halmer and Lin, with a distorted picture for the rest of the cubes.

Tina typed in the date corresponding to the day prior to the beginning of their first cryo-session and selected 0500 on the digital clock. An image of the chambers with all lids up appeared on her display, looking exactly like today's configuration of cubes. She clicked "Next Image," and it popped into view at a camera-time of 50-seconds later. Nothing looked different except for a momentary flicker of light during the change of frames and a new time overlay of 05:00:50.

Then she selected "Time-Lapse," and the image was set in motion. However, since there was no change from frame to frame, only the flicker and the time overlay box told her the day was slowly progressing.

Now Tina entered the next day's date and set the clock to 0500 again. The image remained the same, except for a brighter room light setting. Selection of "Time-Lapse" resulted in no apparent motion. Then, shortly after 0600, the crew began to enter the room, one at a time over the course of the next half hour, appearing as zero-gravity flickering images in the time-lapse views. By 0630, all members of the crew except Cougar and Mercedes were floating near their cryo-beds, with all of their normal clothing removed and now sporting thin, blue hospital gowns. They began attaching semi-transparent blue tape under their armpits and behind their knees and necks, and then connected their own cardiographic surface probes and respiratory umbilical cords. Normally, for a fully-automated hibernation, the Captain would check all of the other cubes with the ship's doctor before taking her position in her own pod. But today that would not be necessary, since Mercedes was remaining awake. So Tina watched herself go through the process with the others, since Don Mercedes would be present to assure all of them went to sleep without problems.

By 0645, all except Kenny Childers were complete with their individual preparations, and he finished up a few minutes later. Doctor Mercedes entered the room at 0652, proceeding from bed to bed, checking everyone's individual preparations and setting the required parameters in their medical recorders. At 0713, crewmembers began to lie down, floating inches above their beds. Each of them stretched for a few minutes to achieve the prescribed position of relaxation. From the overhead camera, everyone could be seen pushing their arms and legs out and cycling them back in, until most of the motion ceased except for the occasional flicker of a hand or foot, and numerous attempts to scratch a final itch on every conceivable spot on their bodies. Someone may have said something particularly funny (the "movies" were without sound), because everyone seemed to move at once, and then finally settled down.

At 0742, Doctor Mercedes floated down the row of cubes, and hit the switches to lower the lids one at a time, beginning with Kenny Childers. In just a few minutes all the lids were closed, except for the cubes belonging to Mercedes and Cougar. Slowly, the clear plastic covers over the beds began to cloud up as the cryogenic cooling took hold. Mercedes remained in the room, gliding from cube to cube, checking medical recorders and occasionally dropping down to verify nano-drug settings. Then, at 0821, Doctor Mercedes pushed himself out the door and was gone. In the following frame, the lights in the room were already dimmed.

Interesting, but not particularly newsworthy, thought Tina, as she fast-forwarded through the following frames. Nothing changed until twelve days later (which consumed over 10 minutes at fast-forward speed) when Mercedes brought Cougar into the cryogenics room after her surgery. Tina reset the cameras to normal time-lapse speed, and watched as Doctor Mercedes stopped the floating gurney at Cougar's cube and helped her slide groggily but weightlessly against the side of the bed. He assisted Cougar with her blue skin patches, cardiographic probes, and respiratory umbilical, for she seemed barely able to raise her arms.

Doctor Mercedes bent down to check a setting on the nano-drug meters at the base of the cube, and then watched as Cougar stretched out in her thin blue hospital gown and tried to find a comfortable position. She raised one arm towards Mercedes, slowly retracted it, and then fell still on her back. She would be entering cryo-sleep in nonstandard format, because of her recent surgery and the steps required when fully automated cryogenics procedures weren't used. Cougar would go to sleep, and Doctor Mercedes would remain on his day-to-day awake cycle for the next five years.

After Cougar was motionless on her bed, Mercedes kept the lid up for a few more minutes. From the overhead camera, Tina could see something impossible to discern in the wall-based view, and in neither camera was it clear how it happened. For two brief frames,

Tina watched as Mercedes looked down at Cougar's body, covered only by the thin hospital gown. The camera didn't catch how his hand moved below her gown to the inside of her thighs, nor did the following frame 50 seconds later show how long it was before his hand returned to a position resting on the bed. In the subsequent frame, the lid of Cougar's cube was halfway down, and three frames later Doctor Mercedes was out the door.

Tina had one more reason to distrust Dr. Donald Mercedes.

* * * * *

TINA NEEDED A FEW minutes to clear her mind and calm down. She turned away from the display and sat in silence until she felt her heartbeat return to normal and her brow clear of sweat. Then she reset the image chronometer for the date during hibernation when Cougar had detected the first sign of deceleration. Setting the clock for midnight and the image selection to "Bridge," she watched the split-screen display that showed a view from the aft wall as well as directly overhead. The top view allowed her to read (at full zoom-in) the digital readings on most of the systems monitors as well as some of the flight instruments. All looked normal as *Challenger* cruised through intergalactic space during the hibernation period.

The readings on the system and flight displays were unchanged, every image looking exactly like the previous one except for the time box and the flicker identifying each change of frame. The "Space Velocity" indicator showed a barely discernible 0.130273 SOL, with a "Max Continuous" prompt below the speed.

Tina watched the images flicker as they changed in time-lapse mode, a new exactly-the-same frame every second and a revised time hack of 50 seconds later on the chronometer. She slid back in her chair and tried to force her eyes to relax as images of the bridge's instrumentation showed steady readings on every gauge. Like the old-fashioned way astronomers once found new planets and asteroids during the twentieth century, she figured her eye would quickly detect any changes as her brain focused on the transition from frame to frame. The biggest problem was the boredom that caused her to gaze around the bridge for a few moments of eye relief and a touch of reality.

After nearly 15 minutes of concentration on the screen, it happened: *Blink. Blink.* Another *Blink.* She hit the "Pause" button, and stared at the velocity indicator. The digits 0.130272 on the velocity indicator didn't catch her immediate attention, but the red overlaid message on the fusion parameters panel had caused the blink. The words in the red box, "Thrust Down," stared back at her.

## Chapter 14

## Houston, We Have a Problem

"Nav, this is the Captain."

"Go ahead, Captain," replied Cougar.

"Would you mind reviewing this fusion drive schematic for me. I sent it encrypted, since that's the way it comes up in the training scenario."

"Sure, I'll give it a look right away."

Tina saw Kenny Childers cock his head sideways at the workstation in front of her, undoubtedly wondering what this was all about. After all, he was the ship's maintenance specialist, in charge of the fusion drive's steady routine.

"Just a training program, Kenny" said Tina, hitting her push-to-talk switch. "Lieutenant Jensen and I are sharing some recurrency software that's supposed to make us more knowledgeable about the ship's subsystems. Part of our on-going training per the mission schedule."

"Oh," said Kenny with a nod. "Let me know if you have any problems understanding the fusion container pressures. It's the toughest part to grasp, but important from a safety standpoint."

"Thanks," replied Tina.

"Captain, this looks like a typical reduced thrust schematic," said Cougar over her headset microphone. "Notice how the 'Thrust Down' annunciator is illuminated, eh?"

Rather than her typical Canadian "Eh?," what Cougar really felt like adding was: "Houston, we have a problem."

And that's exactly how Tina interpreted it.

* * * * *

Cougar fast-forwarded through the frames that Tina sent to her, covering hours of real time in only a few minutes. Ten minutes after the initial deceleration frame with its red "Thrust Down" message, Doctor Mercedes propelled himself weightlessly onto the bridge, and began checking the flight instruments and the fusion drive display. He didn't touch any of the controls (at least in the frames preserved during the playback process), and finally left the bridge after another half-hour of pulling himself from one monitor to another.

This is the confirmation they needed. Obviously, the deceleration had occurred, and Mercedes knew about it. So now the potential conspiracy took scary wings – Doctor Mercedes was lying, and probably so was Major Lin.

It was necessary to act fast but thoroughly, so Cougar called her own image analysis of the second cryo-session back up on her screen, letting Tina continue with the deceleration details of the first hibernation period. She'd already made considerable progress through the jerky "tapes" (a misnomer still widely-used more than 200 hundred years after the last analog tape recording disappeared into history). Cougar quickly returned to the flickering images of the second cryo-session, now at the point where Tina and Mercedes were alone in the cryogenics room after the rest of the crew had begun to enter their second extended period of sleep.

Both were now floating next to their beds. Mercedes' back was to Tina as she slipped out of her clothes, pushed them into the storage container on the floor, and donned a thin blue hospital gown. She attached the required skin tape, cardiographic probe, and respirator umbilical. Then she lay back, stretching out and flexing her legs and arms one last time before entering an immobile position for five years.

Cougar wished Princess could be heard on the tapes, as a clue to the exact timeline involving the hibernation process. The lids of all the other cubes were now closed, with the clear plastic lids enshrouded in various stages of temporary mist. The next frame showed Tina's lid already lowered and beginning to fog, while Doctor Mercedes was now fully prepared for hibernation except for his umbilical and cardiographic probe, seeming about to lay back and begin his hibernation.

Then, in the next flicker of the image, Mercedes was floating towards Tina's cube. In the following image, he was below her chamber, his exact position blocked by the bed of Tina's pod. But this was where the nano-drugs were monitored and injected in situations requiring emergency action. There was no doubt in Cougar's mind what he was doing.

Several more frames flickered with no clearer view of what was happening. Mercedes was floating next to Tina's cube again, and her fogged lid was halfway up. The following image showed the lid fully raised, moisture pouring out on all sides of the bed. In the next several minutes, captured in a few brief images spaced 50 seconds apart in real time and displayed for Cougar ever so briefly, she thought she saw Mercedes' hand on Tina's leg.

Cougar cringed, closed her eyes, and then rewound the "tape." The next time through, she verified that Don Mercedes' hand was on Tina for two frames, and then he was floating beside her again, moisture still pouring out of the cube. In the next frame, the lid was almost fully down, and it was over. Cougar knew she didn't need to see any more to know what was happening. She hit the "Stop" button before Mercedes climbed into his own cube, not wanting to waste any more time watching a psychopathic villain who had callously abused her Captain and dearest friend.

"Captain, can we come back to this systems training a little later today?" asked Cougar over the common bridge frequency. "I've got a bit of a headache."

"Sure," replied Tina, noticing Ken Childers had departed the workstation in front of her while she was engrossed in the deceleration recording. "Let me know if you feel good enough to meet for lunch in the dining room later."

"I'll give you a call," said Cougar, removing her headset and shutting down her display.

"Lieutenant, do you need some meds?" yelled Tim Halmer from the rear of the bridge where he was still playing a video game. He was wearing a headset, but connected to the media sound port, so he shouted a little louder than was necessary to be heard.

"Thanks, Tim!" Cougar yelled back. "I'll be okay."

"See you later," said Tina as Cougar walked past her towards the door at the rear. "Take care of that headache."

Cougar nodded, and then went promptly to their quarters, where rather than taking any pain pills, she activated the entertainment module. And for the first time in years, she began to play a mindless video game.

* * * * *

TINA AND COUGAR ATE lunch together in the dining area, while a baseball-sized spherical microbot with six thin appendages scurried across the counter tidying things up, and then jumped down onto the floor and was gone. They ate silently, not speaking about what they had individually seen that morning, although there was no one else in the room. Their silence said a lot about how they viewed the situation. No one was to be trusted anymore.

When they returned to the bridge, the only occupant was Major Lin, sitting at his normal workstation in the middle row. He started to rise to a slovenly position of attention, when Tina immediately stopped him: "As you were, Major."

"Hello, Captain," said Kim. "Sergeant Childers tells me you're working a systems training program."

"That's right, Kim. It's part of my recurrency training, as spelled out in this week's op-order."

"Didn't see anything about it," said Kim, obviously waiting to hear more.

"The op-order only involves me and Cougar. Just an overview of potential problems with the fusion drive. Nothing to be concerned about."

"Cougar? What does she have to do with it?"

"Well, she's prime in the leadership backup scenario, you know," said Tina, lowering her tone in a way that sounded like she was done with the subject.

"There's nothing wrong with the fusion drive, Captain. And if there was, it's my area of responsibility."

"Of course, Kim. Like I said, it's just a training package. In fact, it's mighty boring. Cougar, would you send me the last training block evaluation, and I'll sign you off on that segment?"

"Sure, Captain," replied Cougar, stepping forward to her bow workstation.

Obviously, Tina didn't want to endure Kim's scrutiny any longer. Major Lin said no more, and returned to whatever he was doing on his screen.

Tina sat down, paused a few moment as she contemplated Kim's reaction, and then activated her workstation. When the screen popped to life, an encrypted message from Cougar was already waiting for her: "I'm done with my part of the project, so I'll start a general scatter-scan on the cameras in the other rooms. Kim is an asshole."

Tina laughed, and Kim looked up momentarily, and then returned to his work. Tina typed a brief reply: "It's hard to tell one from another these days."

\* \* \* \* \*

IN THE PRIVACY OF their quarters that evening, it was a sobering experience for both of the women. Tina offered her report first.

"The images I sent to you pretty much tell the story," said Tina. "I'm still plodding through the deceleration, going slow to make sure I don't miss anything important. The good news is Mercedes doesn't look like he engineered it. He looked mighty surprised when he came onto the bridge right after the deceleration began, looking pretty awkward, partly because he's in zero-G, but with his body movements affected by the deceleration. According to the cameras, as the ship slows, he spends more and more time on the bridge, but I haven't caught him touching a single control. He just keeps monitoring things as the ship decelerates. It sure looks like the fusion drive started throttling back on its own."

"From what I've learned about Mercedes in my little project, it's hard to believe he's innocent. If the fusion drive was acting spontaneously – first of all, I don't see how that could possibly happen – why didn't he try to stop it?"

"Maybe he did try to regain power, but I haven't seen any evidence of it so far. As I said, I'm going slowly, and there's lots of missing images from the compression of the frames. So maybe he's trying to stop the deceleration in ways I can't see. But one thing for sure – Even if he's an innocent bystander, he lied about the situation, and I've seen some other things that are very disturbing."

"Eh?" said Cougar, a clipped and less-laughable version of her Canadian accent.

"Well, this is tough for me to describe to you, and I'm not sure what it has to do with anything…" Tina trailed off, a far cry from her normal disciplined tone.

"Let me guess," said Cougar before Tina could continue. "He's a conspirator, a pervert, and an all-around nasty person."

"How'd you ever guess?" replied Tina, letting out an audible sigh.

"I didn't need to guess. I watched the tapes of the two of you getting ready for hibernation during our second cryo-session. Do you want the details?"

"As a matter of fact, no," said Tina. "Drugs, perversion, or downright lies?"

"All of the above, I'm afraid."

"You're sure about the drugs?" asked Tina.

"No way to tell for sure. But he floated down below your cube after you were asleep, and adjusted something. There's nothing there except the nano-drug monitors and emergency injectors."

"And the perversion?" asked Tina faintly. "I mean was it a real violation or just some senseless touching?"

"There's a lot of missing frames," replied Cougar. "But it was quick and more senseless than anything else."

"Say no more, girlfriend," said Tina, her voice now stronger and determined. "I could tell you about what I saw when he put you to sleep after your surgery, if you want."

"No. I think I can imagine it pretty clearly. Now if I can only forget."

"Well, I don't plan to forget," said Tina. "My Captain's manual warns that vengeance is the worst mistake a leader can make. But in Mercedes' case, I plan to violate all of the rules."

"Here's the tough part," added Cougar. "You'll have to include Kim Lin and who-knows-who-else along with Mercedes. This is getting mighty complicated."

\* \* \* \* \*

While Tina worked on the deceleration frames, Cougar turned her attention to the other rooms on the ship. She looked at hours of images from the dining room, gymnasium, cryogenics area (even when vacant), and the fusion compartment, covering the entire voyage in an AI directed scatter-scan that zeroed in on suspected changes in the images. In the cases of the gym and dining area, the AI targeted nearly every set of frames, since they were high-movement areas.

There were several false alarms that turned out to be routine movements of the crew, so it took a lot of time to wade through. Much had to be skipped, considering the shortage of time until the next Thomson-Jump. After the next 33-light-year leap through space, *Challenger* would be past the point-of-no-return, and they'd have to continue on to Poseidon with whatever conditions existed aboard the ship. It might be a death sentence, and they knew it.

With less than a week remaining until the Thomson-Jump, both Tina and Cougar picked up the pace on their image review, now working alone on the bridge well into the night. The rest of the crew came and went, generally buying into Tina's story regarding their recurrency training. But in two more days, unless the Thomson-Jump was cancelled, both women would need to buckle down to their pre-jump checklists, a series of actions required to slowly reduce the output of the ship's environmental and related subsystems for the pending through space.

Early one evening on the bridge, with Cougar, Tina, and Tim Halmer present (Tim again playing games in the conference area), all was quiet until Tina spoke up over the common frequency.

"Nav, let's wrap it up for the day. I'll see you downstairs."

Tina's tone of voice keyed Cougar into the shades of meaning she sometimes experienced with her closest friend. Tina had found something important, and wanted to get into a private setting to discuss it right away.

"Roger, Captain. I'll start powering things down."

Ten minutes later, in their quarters, Tina blurted out what she had found.

"Okay, you know about the deceleration, and the drift to port side. The ship slowed to a crawl, but never completely stopped. Mercedes was floating around, looking at all the monitors, but not taking control. It looked like he knew he couldn't control the ship, so he just left it alone. During the second day of drifting in a near-dead stop, all hell broke loose on the bridge."

She paused to catch her breath.

"You mean Mercedes starts going ape, or what?"

"No, he was on the bridge, acting all fidgety, pulling himself from monitor to monitor at a frantic pace, just waiting for something. And the next frames show – now, don't laugh! – about a dozen aliens crawling all over everything!"

"Aliens! Holy shit!" exclaimed Cougar, loud enough to break the ice and cause Tina to laugh out loud.

"Well, I'm sure you're gonna' want to see for yourself," said Tina. "So we can check the tapes in the morning, or even later tonight if you want. I'm afraid to send any of the images down here. These media machines aren't secure, and who knows who's watching?"

"Mercedes for one," said Cougar. "And Kim too, I'm pretty sure. But, look, tell me about the aliens!"

"Well, I've just reviewed the first few frames, but the aliens appear suddenly on the bridge. Mercedes tries to scurry off to the side, but they aren't paying any attention to him, just getting in his way as they tromp all over the bridge, moving real quick and touching everything they see. I know they're moving quickly, because each new frame is completely different. None of them stay still for very long."

"They tromp? Tina, what do these things look like?"

"Well, they're rather humanoid, at least closer to humans than any other creature I know, except maybe chimps. Okay, they aren't really 'tromping,' since it's zero-G. But they are rapidly maneuvering with two feet and four arms – two down low that seem to move frantically for balance, and two at shoulder-level that remain relatively idle, but touching this, touching that, and then moving on to reach every cranny in the room. They move so fast it's tough to tell what they're doing. I'm not even sure how many of them are there. I estimate seven, but it's tough to get a clear count because they move and merge all the time. Mercedes looked stunned and desperate, hardly able to catch a breath. You should see his face – it's delightful!"

"Wow!" said Cougar when Tina finally paused to take a breath herself. She waited for Tina to continue.

"So I got through about two real-time hours of images," said Tina as she rushed through her words. "By then my brain was so maxed out I had to quit. That's when I asked you to wrap things up. With Tim there, I just wanted to get to someplace private with you."

"Pirates!" proclaimed Cougar. "It explains our ship's deceleration, but I still don't understand how it happened."

"And I'll be damned if I can figure whether Mercedes was in on it or was just an unlucky Joe who happened to be awake when they arrived."

"Can we go back to the bridge tonight?" asked Cougar.

"Let's wait a few more hours. No one is ever on the bridge after dinner."

"Pirates were one of the original scenarios someone proposed," noted Cougar.

"That was Tim Halmer's input for my list of causes for an unscheduled deceleration of the ship. Maybe the fact he proposed it says something about his loyalties. What do you think, Coug?"

"I like Tim, but I hardly know him. I don't remember seeing him hanging around Mercedes or Kim that much. He spends a lot of time with Kenny, but that's to be expected, since they're the only two enlisted crewmembers, and roommates, too. Tim and Kenny are the only possible supporters we have. We'll need at least one of them if we're going to overcome a big guy like Mercedes or even that runt, Kim."

"Without at least one of them, it's pretty grim," said Tina. "Two girls against four guys, no matter how tough they might be, is a scary thought. Heck, we're starting to talk conspiracy ourselves. What are we coming to?"

"Tina, it's all come down to this, and I think we've seen it coming for some time now. Certainly not the aliens, but we knew Mercedes and Kim are up to no good, whether independently or together. But I keep going back to the fact our entire crew was thoroughly vetted during our initial training, and this mission has been as peaceful as they come. So why would anyone suddenly act up like this?"

"Peaceful, you say?" touted Tina. "I guess you're not including the first aliens anyone from Earth has ever seen. Doesn't seem at all peaceful to me."

## Chapter 15

## Bow Camera

Tina and Cougar waited until well after dinner, knowing no one would normally work that late. They walked through the always-unlocked door to the bridge, and stopped dead in their tracks. In the conference area, only a few meters inside, Mercedes, Lin, and Childers sat at the table, three coffee cups and a plate of nutra-bars in front of them.

"Oh, hi," said Kim, as if it was perfectly normal to be sitting around the table in the bridge late at night, and similarly common for the two women to be going back to work after dinner.

None of the men rose or offered the standard military announcement regarding the Captain entering the bridge, which struck Cougar as very disconcerting. Just an "Oh, hi" to greet their Captain. In all her years with the military, she'd observed comfortable situations where crewmembers began to rise when the Captain entered, and were immediately told: "Carry on," before they even reached their feet. But tonight was an indicator of something very vile that had caused things to deteriorate so fast.

"Hello," said Tina, obviously flustered, but acting as calm as possible.

For Tina and Cougar, it was unsettling just seeing Mercedes so soon after both of them had watched his despicable images in the cryogenics room. Cougar felt her brow grow hot and wet, and felt herself gasping for breath. She felt for Tina, too, but a glance her way said all was under control.

"Just leaving," announced Mercedes. "Kenny was showing us an interesting video game. Neither of us can beat him, so we figure he's cheating."

All three of the men chuckled, although Kenny looked scared. Tina threw them a half-smile, and then continued into the room, Cougar following behind, head down so she didn't have to see Mercedes up close. The men stood to leave, taking their coffee and plate of snacks with them. Their cups were still nearly full, and both computer terminals on the table were in idle mode.

"Good night, Captain," said Kenny, the last man out the door.

When they were gone, Tina was the first to speak.

"We startled them so much that we didn't need to come up with an excuse for being here ourselves. They weren't playing a video game."

"Now what makes you think such a thing, wise leader?" asked Cougar sarcastically.

"Well it does answer one question," said Tina. "At least now we know Childers is in cahoots with both of them."

"Let's hope we still have Halmer," replied Cougar. "Otherwise, we're dead."

\* \* \* \* \*

THE IMAGES WERE UNLIKE anything Cougar had ever experienced. As jerky and time-compressed as the frames were, the aliens were an unexpected dose of reality. Anything so humanoid in stature, but so physically different from the people of Earth, was a shocker.

"Their lower arms seem to just wave around and cause confusion," said Tina as she replayed the actions after the aliens first appeared on the bridge. "If you watch carefully, they get a lot of balance from those arms, moving them quickly to instantly change their center of gravity. Maybe that's why it looks like they're rushing around haphazardly. I think they move so fast because it's easy for them. Don't you think Mercedes looks just as confused as we are?"

"Confused and scared," replied Cougar. "Maybe he knew they were coming, but didn't know how to stop them."

"That's what I think. He might have received a message telling him they were coming – that they'd be slowing the ship down, to make sure he didn't try to stop them."

"So how do you slow a ship down from the outside?" asked Cougar. "I suppose an advanced society could do it, but we sure couldn't."

"No, but it makes sense that Mercedes would have known about their arrival. He was constantly on the bridge, checking the deceleration, but never doing anything to stop it."

"And they left the ship without a single clue they were here, except for the deceleration record in my Nav volume, and now these pictures."

"Don't forget Mercedes keeps reiterating that nothing happened," said Tina. "And Kim almost convinced us there was no surveillance video. Why would they say these things unless they're conspiring with each other and the aliens?"

"But Kim was asleep the whole time," noted Cougar. "And why would two Earthlings, carefully picked for their strengths of character, slip over to the dark side? The aliens, at least as far as we've seen, didn't do anything to our ship except board it without our permission. They left *Challenger* in a fully operational condition, and we'd never have known they were aboard if Mercedes and Lin had successfully covered it up. So what's going on here?"

"Questions, questions. It's too bad your Captain has none of the answers."

"Let's look at some more tape. Maybe we can figure out why they boarded *Challenger* and what they did while they were here. I wonder if there's any way to figure out where they came from, not that it matters, I guess."

"The list seems pretty short," replied Tina. "We know intelligent life is extremely limited, at least in this part of the galaxy. If they came from hundreds of light-years away, what are the chances they would just happen upon our ship? They came here for a specific purpose."

"So who – or what – meets those criteria?" asked Cougar. "That is, who would be fairly close to home?"

"Well they sure as hell aren't from Earth or one of our colonies," said Tina. "Which leaves only one logical place that grabs me."

"Poseidon," said Cougar, nodding in agreement with what she knew Tina was thinking.

"So far, so good," said Tina. "But why would anyone from Poseidon rush out to meet us when we're still only a third of the way to their planet. Even if they wanted to intercept us before we arrive in their solar system, why wouldn't they just wait until we got a lot closer? If they came to annihilate us, they passed up their chance. If it's some kind of greeting, they screwed that up, too."

"Okay," said Cougar, pausing briefly before continuing. "Maybe it's a warning of some kind, like a message saying: 'Go away!' They could have been watching the progress of the *Challenger* project all along, assuming they have the communication capabilities to beat the speed of light, maybe using some form of tachyons or whatever else we haven't invented yet. And probably they don't want to blow us to smithereens. Maybe they just want us to turn around and go home."

"If that's it, then why did they make their intercept so far out from Poseidon?" asked Tina. "Wouldn't it have been more efficient to make direct contact closer to their planet, where the logistics would have been immensely easier? We're headed there anyway, and they must know it."

"Good question. I really can't see any reason, unless crossing the galaxy is so routine for them that they could afford the extra effort and expense, eh?"

"Maybe," replied Tina thoughtfully. "Of course, there are a few other loose ends. Like what do Mercedes and Lin have to do with it? And it would be nice to have some kind of confirmation that these aliens are really from Poseidon."

"I can't explain Mercedes and Lin," said Cougar. "But if these creatures came from Poseidon, we've got a tool to verify that part of the equation."

"Such as?" asked Tina.

"Such as, the fact that visitors from Poseidon would have been coming straight at us for a long time. And we have a camera in our bow that doesn't seem to have much purpose, but it should show a tiny dot growing pretty fast during our first cryo-session."

## Chapter 16

## Blink Test

As interested as Cougar was in the pictures of the aliens, she left the additional viewing to Tina. That provided her with time to dial up the bow camera, and display the forward-looking perspective on her workstation's Nav Scenarios screen. Currently, the view was centered on a nondescript but bright (by comparison) G-class star in Hercules, the home of Poseidon. They were headed almost straight at the star, and it was far brighter than any of the lesser stars in the bow camera view. Poseidon and its sun were still 66 light-years away, but nothing else in the bow view was closer than 100 light-years, including sixteen other naked-eye stars and one barely-visible elliptical galaxy. She wasn't sure how close a spaceship would have to be to be visible in the bow camera, but she was about to find out.

Using the same process she used for her investigation of the images from the second cryo-period, Cougar selected a date a few days before the deceleration, and fast-forwarded through the frames, looking for a tiny object nearly overlain on the bright star in the center. The star itself was considerably dimmer than the current view, since it was photographed before their Thomson-Jump. This should make it easier to see a spacecraft approaching from almost the same position. If the spacecraft could be seen, the offset from the star would be small, but Cougar knew *Challenger's* track wasn't precisely towards the star itself. Their ship's computer was directing them to the point in space where Poseidon would be located at their projected time of arrival, thus slightly offset from the star. Besides, any spacecraft coming straight at them from Poseidon would have launched at a different time of year than *Challenger's* projected arrival date, probably making the planet's offset more notable. All of these celestial deviations should prevent an inbound ship from being completely obscured by the star, at least at close range.

As the frames counted down towards the deceleration, it seemed apparent that no spacecraft was going to appear until after *Challenger* began to reduce speed, which meant either the aliens didn't come from Poseidon or they possessed technology impossible to imagine. If they were able to reduce the thrust in *Challenger's* fusion drive by remote control even before arriving in viewing range, it was through powers no human could understand.

The bow camera images continued well into the deceleration before Cougar stopped fast-forwarding to see if her eyes were playing tricks on her. A tiny gray dot popped out from the background of space, almost right on top of the star in the center of the field of view. At first it was barely visible, dim and minuscule, but she could clearly see it by switching back and forth between the frame where it first appeared and the previous frame. There it is – there it isn't – there it is again. *Blink. Blink.* Another *Blink.* Like the words "Thrust Down" flashing during confirmation of the deceleration, the old-fashioned blink test detected an alien spacecraft inbound from a distant planet.

*****

"Okay, Coug. So how do you explain why they intercepted us so far out?" asked Tina after hearing Cougar's report of the spacecraft image recorded by the bow camera.

"Well, I've been pondering that. One thing for sure, they must know something about how we think. If they can build a spaceship, I'd consider them in an elite group, especially in our neck of the woods. Suppose they know how we think, and they know they need to get to us before we pass the point-of-no-return."

"Why?"

"Well, if they're trying to convince us to turn around and go home, they wouldn't want to wait until after our next Thomson-Jump, which would place us beyond the point-of-no-return."

"Okay, that makes sense," replied Tina. "But how would they know we were even planning a jump?"

"Maybe they have access to our complete flight plan. If they've been watching the development of our mission, they'd know what we were planning and when."

"Speaking of 'when,' doesn't this also means they've been retrieving information from over a hundred light-years away awfully fast?"

"You've got me there, Tina. I've thought about that, too, and I can't see any way they could pull it off unless they're able to receive information faster than the speed of light, which is on the verge of impossible."

"On the verge? Einstein says it's impossible."

"Impossible unless something new and better turns up," noted Cougar. "This society could be so far advanced that they've harnessed faster-than-light technology, at least for communications. Not so far fetched, I'd say."

"No more ridiculous than assuming they have a reason to warn us of something we can't comprehend," stated Tina somewhat ominously. "Something so bad they came all the way across the spiral arm to tell us about it."

"And here's where it gets even muddier," replied Cougar. "Even if they pulled all of this off, why haven't we figured out what they're warning us about? They could have been a lot more straight-forward by just leaving us a note, or saving some Poseidon-bucks and just sending us a message rather than a making a personal visit."

"You're right. There's a clue there, but I can't see it. How did they intend to notify us of their warning, if that's what's going on here?"

"Okay, try this on for size," replied Cougar. "Suppose they really have us figured out. An advanced civilization might have tools allowing them to analyze us – our psyche, maybe even our thoughts. If they really know us, they might conclude nothing would keep us away from their planet, except blowing us up or forcibly turning our ship around. So if we give them the benefit of the doubt regarding humanitarian attitudes, we might conclude they don't want to harm us, but feel they can't convince us to turn around. So they need a way to force us to return to Earth."

"Forcibly?" repeated Tina. "And how do they do that?"

"How about the historic way when it comes to ships at sea, galactic or otherwise. Mutiny works pretty well."

"Meaning?" asked Tina, squinching her cute little lips and simultaneously nodding her head, as if she saw the same possibility as Cougar.

"Meaning, get into the heads of a few key crewmembers, and let it develop from there."

"Mercedes was pretty handy," added Tina. "Wide awake while the rest of us were asleep."

"And once he was on the mutiny bandwagon, he had access to the rest of us while we were sleeping, and for some reason he chose Major Lin and Sergeant Childers, maybe because they're the systems experts. He even tried to get to the ship's Captain during the second cryo-session, but he almost killed you in the process."

"I may be puny, but I'm tough," laughed Tina.

"So what do we do now?" asked Cougar, smiling at Tina's response. "Three strong guys against two puny women and, hopefully, Halmer, if he's really on our side. Not an even match, I'd say."

"But don't forget, girlfriend. We may be puny, but we're tough."

\* \* \* \* \*

THE FOLLOWING FRAMES FROM the bow camera showed the alien spacecraft looming larger as it approached close enough to see a structure similar to the design of *Challenger*, but on a much bigger scale. The craft slowed, and then rode in formation with *Challenger*, the alien ship positioned mostly behind the bow camera, so only the stern was visible, a dull-gray rectangular rear end with hundreds of small orifices that might be propulsion nozzles.

It was soon thereafter, comparing the bow view to the bridge cameras, that the aliens entered and finally settled down after a few hours of what seemed to be aimless "tromping" around. One frame caught them bumping into Mercedes or maybe pushing him aside, although the doctor remained on the bridge (and always in the frames) during the entire 2.7 hours the creatures were present. Then the aliens disappeared from the cameras' view, and were not detected in any of the other onboard cameras, apparently having returned to their ship. After a quiet period of another day, the bow camera recorded the ship's departure. If anything happened to Mercedes during this period, it wasn't recorded by any of *Challenger's* onboard cameras. He had simply disappeared, maybe to his quarters or one of the other image-free areas of the ship.

The day after the alien ship departed, the cryogenics room cameras detected the presence of Doctor Mercedes. The view was disturbing, but not unexpected. Mercedes was observed floating below the cryo-cubes of Major Lin and Sergeant Childers for a few brief moments. Then he exited the cryo-chambers, apparently not attending to the cubes occupied by any of the other crewmembers. However, there were lots of missing frames in the historical record, and it was far from definitive that he didn't adjust the nano-drug settings for anyone else. It did, however, conform to the theory developing within the minds of Tina and Cougar.

What was needed now was a decision about Tim Halmer.

\* \* \* \* \*

Tina and Cougar watched the tapes of the aliens on the bridge over and over, hoping to get further clues regarding why they were there or what they did during their brief stay. The aliens were never captured in the frames shot in the other rooms, and they displayed no weapons or took any action that looked like sabotage or even adjustments to the ship's controls. They weren't seen interacting with Doctor Mercedes, except to casually push him aside when he seemed to be in their path. Basically, the tapes indicated they arrived, floated around the bridge in what seemed an aimless manner, and then departed. Of course, many frames were missing from the recordings in all of the rooms – 49 out of every 50 seconds – so most brief actions went undetected. They could have been in and out of some rooms without ever being captured on tape. And they could have been more involved with Mercedes than was shown in the available frames.

Mercedes' actions in the cryogenic room after the aliens departed were, however, slow and deliberate, involving the cubes of Lin and Childers, and any action near other cubes might not have been caught in the documented frames. Which brought the entire visit by the aliens to a few unsubstantiated conclusions – circumstantial evidence really, involving interaction between the aliens and Mercedes, and his adjustment of the cryo-cubes of at least two crewmembers a few days later. Since Doctor Mercedes seemed to know the foreign ship were coming (based on his activity on the bridge prior to their arrival), there must have been some form of communication with the aliens prior to their arrival aboard *Challenger*. The only way to obtain more facts was from Dr. Donald Mercedes himself. So far, that had been a waste of time.

Tina called Mercedes to the bridge to see what further information she might learn. Cougar and Sergeant Childers were working there at the time, so she asked them to leave in order to talk with Mercedes privately. When they were alone, Tina stared across the conference table at an obviously annoyed Donald Mercedes.

"Don, I need to ask your help in getting this deceleration situation resolved. We really need to put it behind us, don't you agree?"

Mercedes seemed to perk up when she said this, responding with obvious agreement.

"Absolutely, Captain. We've got a mission to accomplish, and all of this talk is getting us nowhere. All of our data says the deceleration never happened, and that's exactly what I witnessed – nothing, nothing at all. If there's something suspect, it's the NavCom data."

"Could be, Don," prodded Tina. "There would have been lots of signs that the deceleration was occurring, including flight monitoring equipment and the general kinesthetic sensations you would have felt. To say nothing of the re-acceleration that would have occurred shortly thereafter."

"I didn't feel anything, and I didn't see anything involving speed changes on the flight monitors."

"Did you go onto the bridge very often during that cryo-period?"

"Once in a while, just to make sure there were no warning lights or anything unusual. Never found anything. Nothing unusual at all."

"What would you say is the longest you ever stayed on the bridge?"

"What is this? – Some kind of inquisition?" replied Mercedes, sounding irritated again.

"No, no. I'm just asking so I can get a sense of your involvement with the bridge, that's all."

"I had no reason to go onto the bridge, although I'd occasionally check the flight monitors."

"Never more than an hour at a time, would you say?" said Tina, pushing the subject.

"Look, Captain, I spent most of my time in my quarters, in the dining area, and working out in the gym. I never spent more than a few minutes – a brief walkthrough – on the bridge. And I didn't see any indications of deceleration or acceleration during the times I was there. Now let's move on to something else, before I call an end to this discussion."

"Don, now please calm down. For one thing – and I hate to have to remind you of this – I'm the Captain, and I'll decide when this discussion is over."

And for another thing, thought Tina, I've caught Mercedes in another lie. If he never spent any prolonged time on the bridge, what about the cameras documenting his pacing on the bridge soon after the deceleration began, to say nothing of the 2.7 hours when both he and the aliens were photographed on the bridge together? Something had to be done about Donald Mercedes, and fast.

## Chapter 17

## Stun guns

"I think you'd do better talking with Sergeant Halmer," said Tina. "I like him, but he seems to be overly cautious when he's around me. Not surprising, considering his enlisted rank. But respect for your Captain seems to have become unreasonably old-fashioned with this crew."

"Which is a good sign when it comes to Halmer," replied Cougar. "Sure, I'll talk to him. Any ideas?"

"See if you can get him to give an honest opinion regarding Mercedes, Lin, and Childers. If we can convince ourselves he's avoiding them, which seems to be the case, it would be a good indication regarding his loyalty. If you say anything about Childers, expect a bit of resistance, because sergeants tend to stick together, especially when they're roommates."

"Sure, I'll give it a try," replied Cougar. "But we really don't have anything on Halmer or Childers, other than the fact that Kenny Childers was at the meeting we interrupted on the bridge."

"Well, there's the camera record of Mercedes messing with Childers' nano-drug panel during hibernation. If we have even an inkling that Kenny has gone over to the other side – which is clearly where Mercedes and Lin reside – we just can't trust him. He could turn on us at any moment, and that's the last thing we need right now."

"And if Halmer has slipped over, too? Then what."

"If we don't have Halmer, it's two puny girls against four angry men, and we're totally fucked," said Tina, speaking a bit un-Captain like, which was enough to cause Cougar to chuckle.

"Not totally fucked," said Cougar, mocking the Captain, which caused a smile to cross Tina's face. "We do have weapons available, eh?"

"Just what we need," replied Tina. "A shootout in deep space."

"I don't want to be too negative here, but we'll also need to take into account that we have a spaceship to run, and doing it without our ship's physician and both of our systems experts is asking a lot. And one more thing – I suppose you've thought about what we're going to do with blatant mutineers, even if we manage to capture them. Put them in chains aboard the ship for a few years?"

"No, aren't you familiar with the informal rules of space travel? We could just chuck them out where'd they do no harm."

"Sometimes, my dear Captain, I truly can't tell when you're kidding."

\* \* \* \* \*

Sergeant Tim Halmer and Lieutenant Cougar Jensen met in private at the same conference table where Tina had accomplished so little with Mercedes. Cougar hoped this meeting would be more productive.

"Tim, the Captain asked me to meet with you, but I want to make sure you know what I'm about to discuss with you is in concert with her desires. She respects you a lot, but she thought you'd feel more comfortable with me, so here I am."

"I'm not in some kind of trouble am I?" asked Halmer, with a sincere sense of concern.

"Should you be?"

Halmer thought for a moment, and then laughed: "Nah. I guess not."

"You're not in any trouble," said Cougar, trying to set him at ease. "But we need to look into some things that have been going on lately, and Tina thinks you might be able to help. That's all, okay?"

"Sure, Cougar, er... Lieutenant. I'd like to help with... well, whatever it is."

"Good. So you can start by calling me Cougar, like you usually do."

"Thanks," replied Tim, obviously a bit relieved. "What would you like to know?"

"Well, for starters, have you noticed our military professionalism seems to be slipping a bit lately? I'm not talking about you – just talking in general terms."

"I hate to say anything about... about any of the others," stammered Halmer.

"Sure, I understand, Tim, but the Captain has come up with a problem we all need to help her solve."

"What's that?" asked Tim, sounding suspicious.

"Well, have you noticed there are a lot of complaints lately from Doctor Mercedes and Major Lin? The Captain is concerned there might be some underlying problems needing attention. What do you think?"

"I've tried to stay out of it," replied Tim. "Kenny has been after me to meet with some of the crewmembers who have complaints about conditions aboard the ship, but I haven't joined any of their meetings."

"You mean meetings involving Doctor Mercedes, Major Lin, and Sergeant Childers?"

"Well, I know there's something going on between them, but I've kept out of it. Kenny and I are friends, but I'd rather not get involved in anything that's not arranged by the Captain."

"Good decision, Tim. I don't mean to press you on this, but it could become pretty serious, if proper action isn't taken."

"Well, I know Kenny thinks Doctor Mercedes and Major Lin have some valid complaints about our conditions, but I don't see it myself. The biggest problem is that they're talking behind the Captain's back."

"You're right, Tim. That isn't a good thing, and the Captain may need your support to get things back on track."

"What can I do?" asked Tim, sounding incredulous that he could assist. "I mean, I'll do whatever the Captain asks, but I don't want to piss off the reset of the crew. Oh, sorry, Lieutenant. My language wasn't appropriate there."

"No problem, Tim. Both the Captain and I may be about to take a big chance on you, and you're more important in all of this than you think. You do realize the talk you're hearing from Mercedes, Lin, and even Sergeant Childers is on the verge of a mutinous discussion."

"Mutiny?" said Tim, his face scrunched in an uncomfortable pose. "I thought they were just grumbling about things. It seems to happen on almost every mission I've been on, but nothing has ever come from it."

"Maybe it's different this time," said Cougar.

"If that's what the Captain thinks, then tell her I'll do whatever she wants."

"Good, Tim. That's what I thought you'd say. We're probably going to need you, so stay alert, and let me or the Captain know about anything you observe that indicates the situation is getting worse."

"Sure, Cougar. I worked hard to get on this mission, and I don't want to screw it up now. You're not thinking of turning around and heading back to Earth, are you?"

"Well, we're thinking about it. But if I know our Captain, you can count on her to do everything possible to complete this mission just like it was planned."

"Which means another Thomson-Jump in just a few days," observed Tim.

"Sure. We're already starting the pre-jump checklists. But we may have to take care of this dissention first, so be prepared, if we ask."

"That I will. You can count on me," said Tim with a sense of pride.

Cougar hoped she could count on him. Having put nearly all the cards on the table with Tim Halmer, there weren't a lot of options left.

\* \* \* \* \*

OVER THE NEXT FEW hours, Tina and Cougar planned their attack on Mercedes, Lin, and Childers. Their only hope was to catch them by surprise while they were together. One thing for sure, if they faltered, there wouldn't be a second chance. If given the slightest opportunity to retaliate, these three men could easily overpower Tina, Cougar, and Childers, with or without weapons. However, with a surprise attack and the advantage of the two onboard hunting weapons, designed for self-defense from animals in a planetary natural environment, they stood a chance. The two stun guns weren't meant for use on aliens or humans. The project team considered the remote possibility of alien hostilities to be an immediate lose-lose situation, with only six humans on the mission. The issue of intergalactic pirates was dismissed as outrageously unlikely, and an onboard mutiny could be made worse by the availability of lethal weapons. So they departed Earth with two nearly-harmless small pistols, stored for safety in a locked cabinet, accessible only through the simultaneous touch of two personal ID tags. To call them stun guns was an accurate description.

"I never fired them in training," noted Cougar.

"Neither did I, although they're supposed to fire like conventional pistols," replied Tina. "But with hardly any kick. Temporary immobilization is all we can expect."

"Like a cop's stun gun?" suggested Cougar.

"The same, and police have never used them with great success in stopping criminals. We'll only get one chance. They're entirely manual by design, so we won't have time to pull the trigger more than once if we're at close range. So make the first shot count."

"What about damage to the hull?" asked Cougar.

"Not a problem. It's only a high voltage pulse, although they were meant to be used in a planetary forest. No one intended them to be fired aboard the ship, that's for sure."

"Stunted, unsuccessful, and not designed for what we need," noted Cougar. "Sounds perfect for the job."

"Perfect is a relative term, Coug. We're all untested on this, so we'll take what we can get."

"So who gets the guns?" asked Cougar. "I've never been much to brag about on the firing range. And that was with a real firearm. So maybe you and Tim should handle the guns."

"No, you and I will take the pistols. Tim still isn't a known quantity, and there's no way we're gonna' know about him until the time comes. If he's on the other side, giving him a gun could end it before we even get started. Besides, we're going to need to rely on him for brute force, what there is of it."

"The Three Mouseketeers," said Cougar. "Outta' our way – here come two chicks and a male nurse to the rescue." Cougar stopped, and then laughed, making sure Tina didn't interpret it the wrong way. Then she added: "Gonna' kick some ass."

"Kick or kill," said Tina. "Whatever it takes to get these guys down long enough to get them tied up. You can't go to prison if the wardens aren't in control."

"Oh, maybe you noticed – nobody ever built us a prison, so that might be a problem, especially with at least ten years to go, even if we Thomson-Jump all the way home."

"Actually, they did build a prison for us," said Tina. "Call it a multi-purpose room. Or you can call it the cryo-cubes."

\* \* \* \* \*

THEIR PLAN, SUCH AS it was, was laid out by Tina during the one-and-only meeting between Cougar, Tim, and Tina. They met in the unlocked conference room, ready to break up their meeting immediately if anyone walked in, claiming their session involved health considerations for the crew during the upcoming Thomson-Jump. But no one interrupted their conversation, Tina keeping the briefing short and to the point.

"Tim, I'm asking you to accept what we're about to do, without time for much explanation. Mercedes, Lin, and Childers are risks to the completion of this mission, and we have to subdue them. We need to act immediately, before they have a chance to overpower us first. Then, once we have them in custody, we'll discuss how to handle the mission without them."

"Right, Captain. Lieutenant Jensen briefed me on your concerns. The only thing I need to know is whether you want me to consider this a lethal attack."

"I'd prefer that no one is killed or even seriously injured, Tim. But it's essential we subdue all three of them as quickly as possible. If it takes deadly force, so be it."

"Understood, Captain. Do you want me to advance on them once you have them at gunpoint?"

"I remind you it's only stun guns, and they'll recognize that right away. So we'll need you to move in and get them cuffed, hands first, and then feet. We'll instruct them to get down on the floor immediately, but you'll have to work quickly with the ropes and tape."

"You can count on me, Captain," said Tim.

If they couldn't, it would be all over before it even got started.

\* \* \* \* \*

TINA CALLED A MEETING of all crewmembers, using the pretext of preparation for the Thomson-Jump. She used the bridge's overhead camera to watch from her quarters, while Cougar sat nearby on her upper bunk. They watched as Sergeants Childers and Halmer arrived first, plopping down at the conference table, followed a few minutes later by Doctor Mercedes and Major Lin. Once the four of them were in place, Tina and Cougar made their way to the bridge, arriving only a minute before the scheduled meeting time. They walked in with their pistols already drawn, Tina quickly yelling: "No one move!"

As planned, Tim Halmer stood up immediately and pulled the table back towards the wall, and then stepped to the side, away from the other three men, while Tina yelled the next command: "Down on the floor, right now!"

There was a brief moment when no one moved, and then Doctor Mercedes rushed towards the table, trying to pull it down in front of him as a shield. Cougar didn't hesitate, firing at him immediately, hitting him high in the chest, near his neck. Even with only a stun gun, she could have killed him, but she didn't care. Quickly, her finger was back on the trigger, ready to fire again, although it would take the weapon a few moments to recharge itself.

"Down on the floor! Now!" yelled Tina.

Mercedes was already hunched over on his side, behind the table, his knees pulled to his chest. Childers and Lin slid down off their chairs, as instructed. Tim Halmer rushed forward to begin tying up Childers and Lin first. Meanwhile, Cougar kept her pistol aimed at Mercedes, while Tina focused on the other two.

Doctor Mercedes lay motionless until Tim Halmer completed the cuffing of the hands of Childers and Lin. Then he rushed over to Mercedes, and cuffed his hands and feet, too. Then back to the other two to complete the cuffing of their feet.

"Fucking women," said Major Lin without a hint of emotion.

"Fucking done with you," replied Tina, dropping the aim of her weapon to the floor. And then she smiled.

Chapter 18

**1420 Megahertz**

THREE PEOPLE – HALF OF the original crew – remained to run the ship. Leadership and navigation were intact, and medical responsibilities were fully covered by Tim. The only badly fractured link was systems expertise, but *Challenger's* flight manuals were enough to get by for years, unless something broke. Then they would simply have to work together to get it fixed.

Donald Mercedes wasn't seriously injured by the stun gun, although it left a severe bruise on his upper chest. With Mercedes, Childers, and Lin fully drugged by Tim Halmer, they dragged the bodies from the bridge to the cryogenics room. Following flight manual procedures for putting part of the crew into deep freeze, they had the three troublemakers out cold by late evening. The cryo-lids were closed, the nano-drugs established, and a wakeup date set for "Indefinite." The crisis was over, and Tina and her reduced crew could give their attention to what they should do with the ship. For the time being, they elected to delay the Thomson-Jump at least a few more days until they decided whether they wanted to cross the point-of-no-return. They were far behind in their preparation for the jump anyway, and who knew if it should even occur under current conditions.

"First things first," said Tina, as they sat around the dining table, finishing their evening meal. "Now that we can take a deep breath without looking over our shoulders, I think it's time for a bit of a ceremony."

She reached into her pocket and brought out the cloth-on-velcro lieutenant bars she had asked Cougar to prepare for her. They were marked over in colored pen so Cougar's white bars were now light brown, appropriate for a second lieutenant.

"We had agreed to retain our current ranks for the entire voyage," said Tina. "But this is something unforeseen. With Sergeant Halmer's new responsibilities over the medical side of the house, especially considering his actions in helping us through this mess, I'm using my authority as mission commander to make a field promotion. Sergeant, please stand and prepare for commissioning as an officer in the Space Force of the North American Union."

Tim Halmer didn't know how to react to this, but when both Tina and Cougar stared at him, he popped up quickly and stood firmly at attention.

"By the power vested in me by the Unified Nations in Space, I hereby promote Sergeant Timothy Halmer to the rank of second lieutenant in the Space Force of the North American Union."

Tina approached Tim face-to-face, and he saluted her immediately. She returned the salute, and said: "At ease, Lieutenant Halmer."

Tina removed Tim's NCO chevrons from their velcro holders, and secured the cloth brown bars in their place. Tim's face glistened red, and he smiled with pride. Cougar came forward to offer him her hand, and he shook it exuberantly. Then Tina did the same, and he clasped it tight, hanging on for a moment.

"Congratulations, Lieutenant."

"Wow, does that ever sound good!" replied Tim.

It was a fine way to get back on track for all of them, but Tina asked Cougar and Tim to remain for a few minutes before they retired to their quarters.

"Here's some things I need you to think about," said Tina. "Unless we're stupid enough to wake up Mercedes and try to interrogate him further, we'll need to use whatever indirect evidence we can find to determine what went on when the aliens came to visit. We'll probably never know for sure, but maybe there's a way to figure out how they communicated with Mercedes, and what they said. Most important, if they issued a warning to him, we need to find out what they planned to accomplish, and how they went about it.

"Also, if we decide to proceed with the Thomson-Jump rather than turn tail and head home, we'd better be as sure as possible what we're getting into. Any ideas before we break for the night."

"Just the obvious," said Cougar. "It seems to me the aliens were determined to use Mercedes, Lin, and Childers as pawns to turn *Challenger* around. What else could have been the purpose of a mutiny? But if that's the case, it means we're dealing with a benevolent advanced civilization clearly capable of stopping us in our tracks an easier way. With everyone asleep except Mercedes, they could have blown us up rather than going to all the trouble of creating a mutinous scenario. But they chose to let us live."

"So if it was their way of warning us not to continue, they elected to do it passively rather than aggressively," said Tina. "Still, they must know that our returning home wouldn't end it for them. We – and they – recognize that an aborted mission this time wouldn't stop human beings from pursuing the goal of reaching Poseidon. In fact, if they understand us like they seem to, they'd know it would make Earth's desire to reach Poseidon even more intense. So why would they come all this way to mess with us?"

"Yes, it seems more like a delay tactic than an ominous warning," replied Cougar.

"Any ideas, Lieutenant?" asked Tina.

It took Tim a brief moment to realize she was talking to him: "Oh, no, nothing," he stammered, as he suddenly realized he was a lieutenant – one of only three officers who would work together to make a very important decision. They were still 15 years from the point-of-no return, but in a single Thomson-Jump, they would be well on the other side, and committed to Poseidon.

"Well, as I said, give it some serious thought," said Tina to Cougar and Tim. "And if either of you comes up with an idea regarding how we can determine what happened between Mercedes and these unusual creatures, let me know right away, even if it's the middle of the night."

In reality – and all three of them knew it – it was always the middle of the night during this mission. And it would remain that way until they reached a planet, either Earth or Poseidon.

\* \* \* \* \*

"Hey, girlfriend. I need you to wake up," said Cougar in her sometimes-mischievous voice.

Tina pulled her blanket down, trying to bring herself awake. The chill of the night air helped pull her out of the daze of sleep. This might be an emergency, or maybe Cougar needed some love. Either was important, but she could barely focus for a few seconds.

"Coug, what is it?" she said, trying to talk herself awake, rolling over to face the open side of her bed. Cougar sat in the straight-backed rocker, smiling at her. It wasn't an emergency, so maybe Cougar really did need some love.

"Sorry, Tina, but you said to do it. Wake you up, that is, if I came up with something. I can't say I dreamed it, but it's rather brilliant, if you ask me."

"I'm asking," replied Tina, now awake enough to sit up on the side of her bunk. Cougar was dressed in her light blue pajamas, hands resting on her knees in front of the chair, with a wide grin now crossing her face.

"If we need to find out what the aliens said to Mercedes, we could just ask," said Cougar.

"Okay," replied Tina, looking more alert. "But it could be dangerous to wake him up, and he hasn't been exactly cooperative so far."

"No, no. Not Mercedes. We ask the aliens. I'm your NavCom, you know, so I know something about communicating in space."

"I didn't know you were well versed in alien-speak," said Tina in an attempted joke that came over flat in her middle-of-the-night stupor.

"Well, my alien-speak sucks. But I bet they know English-speak. They seem to know everything else about us."

"Right. Well, why not? Yes, let's get right at it, Coug. I guess we could just shout as loud as we can, since we don't have a clue what radio frequency would work. Have you thought about how we'd get their attention?"

"Sure. Anything should work to get things started," said Cougar. "How about: 'What the hell is happening, eh?'"

"They might not speak Canadian," laughed Tina. "And I'm sure you've thought about the time delay in this miraculous idea."

"It might be a long shot, but radio waves are free. Sure, if our signal has to go all the way to Poseidon, it's probably a dead end. But they may have speed-of-light limitations figured out, at least for communications. Or better yet, the ship that visited us may be hanging around waiting for us to make our next move. So we might get a response to a message right away."

"Since I now realize you're serious, it's worth a try," said Tina, still a bit groggy. "Would you let Tim know so he can get up early and meet us for a brief meeting before breakfast? Meanwhile, your Captain will go back to sleep for a few more hours."

"The privileges of command," laughed Cougar. "Sweet dreams, girlfriend."

\* \* \* \* \*

"This is spaceship *Challenger*, transmitting in the blind to any vessel in the vicinity," said Cougar over the microphone, as Tina and Tim looked on. "*Challenger* is an Earth-based ship en route to a planet we have designated as 'Poseidon,' with no evil intentions and a request for assistance. *Challenger* will be standing by on this frequency, 1420 megahertz, for a reply."

The transmitting channel was a best-guess, based on the universal 1420 megahertz hydrogen emission frequency which had been used (unsuccessfully) for centuries in the search for extraterrestrial intelligence. Still, it was the best attention-getter known to man. Simultaneously, *Challenger* transmitted Cougar's message on a variety of other LF and UHF channels that were nothing but statistically-spread stabs in the dark. Only 1420 megahertz had any logic behind it. For reception, the ship set one of its receivers to this frequency, while three other radios scanned wide bands of the electromagnetic spectrum in LF, UHF, and VHF.

There was nothing to do but repeat the message over and over again, and sit back and wait. And then wait some more.

Meanwhile, the crew prepared for the next Thomson-Jump. Powering down the ships systems was necessary, while Cougar ran her navigation checklists in conjunction with Tina. Tim Halmer was assigned systems maintenance training, using the ship's computer, since both Major Lin and Sergeant Childers were in cryo-sleep. It was anticipated the three mutineers would remain in sleep mode for the remainder of the voyage, whether the destination was Poseidon or a return to Earth. For now, since their destination wasn't yet firmly decided, they ran the pre-jump checklists without a direction specified.

Once the jump was complete, Cougar would also tackle some systems training. Although her preparation would be less extensive than Halmer's, it would be good to have two qualified maintenance specialists ready in case of any problems with the ship.

For the Thomson-Jump checklists, a specific transition date had to be established, and Tina selected a day and time in the following week, knowing it might need to be changed or even cancelled. It was good to get back to normal as far as ship operations were concerned, taking their attention away from the stress that had been nearly nonstop since the deceleration event was detected. Tina's crew, now decreased by half, thrived on the tasks-at-hand, and the mood rapidly changed from sustained anxiety to enthusiastic preparation for the next portion of their flight plan, whatever direction they might travel.

*****

THREE DAYS AFTER THEY transmitted their message to the aliens, a reply was received over the HF radio link. It was in plain English, clear and concise – a male voice sounding thoroughly human, although the message came through in the typical in-a-tunnel tone that was common in the HF band, the voice rising and fading, similar to the way an HF signal bounced off the Earth's atmosphere. Nearly invisible interstellar clouds of gas had a similar effect on the communication beam.

"Spaceship *Challenger*, this is spaceship *Gardenpeace*, replying to your request for assistance. We're currently four light-days away, and powering up as quickly as possible for rendezvous with your ship. We estimate arrival in approximately six Earth-days. Stand by for further information."

Tina, alone on the bridge when the call arrived, made an excited reply.

"Spaceship *Gardenpeace*, this is *Challenger*. We're receiving you loud and clear. Standing by, as requested."

"*Gardenpeace*, roger." The short reply seemed low in enthusiasm but high in professional tone. "Please begin a speed reduction to one percent SOL in preparation for docking."

"*Challenger*, roger. We understand your request."

Which was an efficient way to make a reply, since Tina did understand what they were asking, but she wasn't sure her crew would comply. But it would give her time to think.

She immediately summoned Cougar and Tim, and in just a few minutes, they were both at their workstations, Cougar at the bow, and Tim in the seat between the two women, where Don Mercedes used to sit.

"Talk about historic!" bubbled Cougar after Tina replayed the radio conversation. "First communications contact with an alien intelligence, and now we're headed for a face-to-face encounter."

"Don't forget...," replied Tina. "It's been done before, except we were asleep at the time. Mercedes probably communicated with them before they arrived, and he definitely met with them in person."

"I'll never tell," joked Cougar. "One small step for womankind. Do you think we should make a follow-up transmission?"

"Let's wait and see what happens," replied Tina. "To me, it sounded like they were merely briefing us on their planned rendezvous. Listen again."

Tina hit the replay button, and Tim and Cougar listened in awe a second time.

"Four light-days away and six days to get here is interesting, don't you think?" asked Tim. "They can travel at nearly the speed of light."

"Or maybe they're using a space jump that's a lot more accurate than ours," replied Cougar. "So far, everything we know about them says they're far more advanced than we are."

"Which also means we need to be careful," said Tina. "They haven't done anything directly hostile yet, but two gals and a guy wouldn't be much of a match."

"So we wait?" said Cougar.

"Right, Coug. We start slowing down, and let them play this out however they decide. We definitely need to remain on the defensive, but we'll follow their plans, at least for now. Unless either of you has an objection?"

Nobody said anything, so Tina continued: "Okay, Tim, can you get us started on the deceleration checklist."

"Done!" replied Tim, immediately turning to his workstation display.

And so they cancelled their pre-jump preparations, and began running the deceleration checklist. They were plenty busy, which was a lot better than just waiting as patiently as possible. While Tim and Cougar ran the checklist, Tina did what they hired her for – she sat at her workstation and thought about what was to come.

* * * * *

THE NEXT AFTERNOON, AFTER receiving no further transmissions from *Gardenpeace*, Tina asked Cougar to attempt another radio contact.

"*Gardenpeace*, this is *Challenger*. Radio check."

The reply was immediate.

"*Gardenpeace* reads you loud and clear. Stand by for docking information as soon as we have it available. We note your deceleration rate, and it appears well within our docking parameters."

"Meaning what?" asked Cougar over her hot-mike link to Tina and Tim.

"Meaning… they really aren't ready to talk right now," replied Tina. "Okay, we'll let it ride," said Tina. "They've got their communications lingo down pat, but I'm getting tired of the phrase 'Stand by.' We'll split our shifts so the bridge is continually manned to monitor the deceleration and in case our friends decide to call us."

"We're not equipped for ship-to-ship docking," noted Cougar. "How do you think they plan to pull it off? They seem pretty matter-of-fact about it."

"Probably the same way any civilization substantially more advanced than ours would handle things – magic," said Tina. "Europeans must have seemed like they used magic when they arrived in North America. Huge ships, weapons that burst with fire, you name it. It's always been that way in history when vastly different civilizations collide, so we shouldn't be surprised. The difference this time is we're on the receiving end."

"Which usually isn't the best end," added Cougar. "Consider North America's original natives, disease and decimation included."

* * * * *

Lieutenant Tim Halmer was alone on the bridge when *Gardenpeace* made its next contact, the clock winding down for rendezvous.

"*Challenger*, in preparation for docking, please continue your speed reduction to one percent SOL. If you can slow to that speed within the next 30 hours, it will work out fine from our standpoint."

"Roger, *Gardenpeace*. I'll pass this on to our Captain immediately. We're continuing with our deceleration, and estimate reaching one percent SOL within 17 hours. Do you want us to continue decelerating beyond that target speed?"

"Negative, that won't be necessary, *Challenger*. Our ship is certified for docking at a mutual speed of one percent SOL. You may prefer to retain that forward speed to expedite your departure. We understand your acceleration from a stopped condition is a lengthy process. *Gardenpeace* out."

Well, that's pretty abrupt, thought Tim. But there seemed to be two good pieces of information here. First, it sounded like the aliens consider the upcoming docking a routine maneuver. Better yet, they indicated that *Challenger* was expected to leave the scene of the docking under its own power.

Maybe even more encouraging was the satisfaction Lieutenant Tim Halmer felt from being solely in charge of this contact with an alien ship. Last week, as a lowly sergeant wondering whether he would survive an impending mutiny, he had been on the verge of panic. Today, he was sitting at the Captain's station, fulfilling his assigned duties as an officer in the Space Force of the North American Union, and communicating with aliens as the officer-in-charge. Even if it was only for a brief period, it simply didn't get any better than this.

He called Captain Brett at her quarters immediately, filling her in on the communication contact. She was on the bridge a few minutes later, listening to the audio record.

"Well done, Lieutenant. They signed off rather rudely, but no fault of yours. What was your overall impression when you were talking to them?"

"It felt like they were talking down to me, especially the part about our acceleration limitations. But maybe that's more of a language translation flaw, since they're obviously not fluent in English."

"So you don't think they studied it in school?" joked Tina.

"That's for sure. When you think about the situation, it's totally amazing they can communicate with us so clearly. I guess I shouldn't be critical of their style."

"No, no. You're perfectly correct. They do sound condescending, although it's obvious they have capabilities far in advance of ours. But it's right for you to be listening to their tone, since it's our best way to judge what's going on here."

"They actually sound concerned about our slow acceleration capability," said Tim. "And it made me think they aren't planning to hold us hostage. Otherwise, why would they mention our departure?"

"Another valid point," replied Tina. "And we'll take them up on their suggestion. Set our speed control for steady at one percent SOL, no slower, and closely monitor the final deceleration."

"Aye, aye, Captain," replied Tim in the exaggerated old-military style.

The Captain was on the bridge – her bridge – and she was letting Tim continue to operate the ship. When he recognized what she was saying, he realized it had just gotten even better.

Cougar stepped onto the bridge a few seconds later, and Tina said: "Listen to this, Coug."

After hearing the replay of the communications, Cougar smiled, and said simply: "It sounds like we're a child, needing a little discipline."

"Great minds think alike," replied Tina with a smile. "All three of us."

## Chapter 19

### Rendezvous

Two days later, with all three of the crewmembers on the bridge, Cougar received an automated alert from the ship's radar. She broadcast the results over the hot-mike to Tina and Tim.

"Radar contact, one hundred and twelve kilometers southeast, closing at a relative speed of point-zero-zero-two SOL. Will be here in a few seconds!"

"Must be huge, for us to paint a target so far out," replied Tina. "How will they slow in time?"

"Already down to almost nothing – both relative speed and distance. Too bad we don't have a rear-mounted camera."

They didn't need one. A moment later, the front of a steel-gray ship poked into the bow viewport, slowing to a crawl as it slid forward and rode in formation, an immense windowless structure taking up the whole right side of the viewport, seeming to revolve slowly around them, an effect of their own rotation. The alien ship ended in a blunt nose, with a slightly bulbous raised area a short distance from the front. There were no noticeable markings of any kind.

The ship had come in quickly from the southeast (meaning their starboard side, closing from behind), and now floated next to them in space. Since *Challenger* was still in its normal rotational mode for standard gravity, the alien ship was moving slowly up and over them. Cougar pushed her nose up against the bow window, trying to look back to view more of the ship, but there was no end as far as she could see.

"Hello. You might have given us a little more warning," said Tina sarcastically over their own hot mike.

"Another indicator they don't consider us their equals," replied Cougar. "Or maybe they just don't know what common courtesy is about."

"Do you think they might be trying to catch us off-guard, sneaking up by surprise?" suggested Tim.

"Not with that big snout sticking out in front of us," said Cougar. "Let me try to contact them."

"Go ahead," said Tina. "Let's try to act like we consider ourselves their equals, or at least worthy of some dialogue."

"*Gardenpeace*, this is *Challenger*, over," transmitted Cougar.

"*Challenger*, we're now preparing for entry to your ship. This will only take a few minutes, so you can plan to meet us on your bridge. Are you aware of our physical appearance?"

Interesting question, thought Cougar, looking back at Tina for some guidance. It didn't sound like the aliens knew the *Challenger's* crew had seen images of them or had indirect knowledge of their appearance, which was a good sign. If the brainwashing theory was correct, maybe the aliens had no idea whether Doctor Mercedes was successful in his attempt to takeover the ship.

Tina nodded to Cougar, implying she should tell the aliens they knew what they looked like.

"Roger, *Gardenpeace*. We are aware of your appearance, and we understand you are aware of ours."

"Excellent, *Challenger*. We know it would take you some time to get used to our physical attributes, as it was originally difficult for us to accept your characteristics. Our society has had a lot longer to absorb the situation, and we respect your challenges in this area."

Two things, thought Cougar immediately: it sounds like these aliens have known about humans for some time; and at least, they know the word "respect."

Cougar didn't even need to turn to Tina this time or ask her instructions. She suddenly knew what she needed to say.

"*Gardenpeace*, we need to get a few things straight before you come aboard. On our world, we don't just enter another vessel without getting permission from the Captain. Second, if you come aboard our ship, you will be our guests, and shall be treated as such. However, we also expect you to respect our sovereignty, and act by our rules while aboard."

Unlike all of her previous transmissions to the alien ship, there was no immediate answer. In fact, it remained strangely silent.

Cougar now turned to Tina, who was smiling broadly and nodding her head: "Maybe they need a dictionary for 'sovereignty,'" said Tina, "Or you simply caught them dumbfounded."

"*Challenger*, this is *Gardenpeace*," the voice said slowly.

"Yes, go ahead *Gardenpeace*."

"Our Captain sends his apologies for our overly forceful words. We are new to your language. Captain Yeleng-Kan asks your kind permission to come aboard."

When Cougar turned around, Tina was smiling and pumping both fists in the air.

"Roger, *Gardenpeace*. Captain Brett of the spaceship *Challenger* acknowledges your request, and invites you aboard."

"Thank you," replied a humble-sounding voice.

"Upon entry, please report to the bridge. We look forward to meeting you. We can prepare our ship now to terminate our rotation in preparation for your entry."

"Roger that. Captain Yeleng-Kan appreciates your approval of our request. However, there is no need to cease your vessel's rotation in preparation of our boarding. *Gardenpeace* out."

Cougar took off her headset, and stood up. Tina and Tim were also putting their headsets aside, appearing more confident than they'd looked for a long time.

"That's quite a victory," said Tina. "But it gets pretty spooky when you realize they know how to get into our ship without us activating any of our exterior hatches. And they plan to do it while we're still rotating."

"Do you want me to go down to see what's going on?" asked Tim.

"No, we'll just stay here, and wait. Seeing them for real is still going to be quite a shock. So let's try to calm down the best we can. My guess is they'll be aboard in only a few minutes."

"With your permission, of course," laughed Cougar.

"Hey, we've gotta' start somewhere," replied Tina.

\* \* \* \* \*

As many times as they'd seen their photos, it was still unnerving when the aliens entered the bridge. There were five of them, and they moved brusquely, seeming in a rush to investigate everything in the room. Yet they'd been here before.

It wasn't clear who was in charge, all five of them moving through the entry door and bypassing the three humans now standing next to the conference room table. They darted in separate directions, moving quickly, leaning over the monitors and controls, but not touching a thing. Their lower arms waved back and forth in clipped motions as they moved, while their upper arms were relatively motionless. It was more of a bouncing movement than a walk, and they kept at it for a few minutes. Then they abruptly settled down all-at-once, and walked slowly back to the conference table to face the humans. The five aliens bowed slowly in recognition, and the three humans acknowledged them by following suit.

Tina waved her arm towards the table, and one of the aliens pulled a chair out and sat down. The other four remained standing behind him.

Tina took her seat across from the aliens, motioning to Tim and Cougar to follow suit. The alien who was now sitting, staring at them with huge gray eyes, offered the first words anyone had spoken since their brisk arrival.

"I am Captain Yeleng-Kan. I'm pleased you agreed to meet with us."

The Captain's voice was deeper than the representative who had been communicating with them on the radio. It was an aggressive voice, sounding like it belonged to an individual clearly in charge and used to getting his way.

"And I'm Captain Brett, pleased to make your acquaintance. Welcome to our ship."

"It's very impressive," said the Captain. "We're intrigued with all of the monitoring equipment you use to control your ship. *Gardenpeace* has far fewer controls."

Captain Yeleng-Kan looked and sounded very masculine. His stature was slightly smaller than a human, but his facial features were amazingly humanoid, with bigger eyes, slightly larger ears, and a human-like nose. Each of his four hands had four fingers and a thumb, covered with medium-toned skin. He wore a trendy-looking gray tunic that covered everything except his two sets of hands and his head, which was capped with thin hair worn in a style similar to a crew-cut. Of course, the two extra lower arms caught the attention of *Challenger's* crew, and the upper arms seemed a bit shorter than most humans. Looking at Yeleng-Kan and the others was less of a shock than the human crew had expected. And it certainly helped that they spoke English.

Tina decided to take the offensive, trying to establish her stance before an obviously superior intelligence. She intended to stand her ground regarding the aliens' disturbing and secretive first visit.

"We were able to use onboard cameras to view your previous visit to our ship," said Tina. "We're concerned with your actions involving boarding our vessel while the main contingent of our crew was in cryogenic hibernation."

"The human we contacted wasn't in hibernation. Where is he now?"

"He and two others are being held as prisoners," stated Tina, waiting for the meaning to sink in.

"I see," replied Yeleng-Kan. "We didn't know you were in a cryogenic state when we boarded your ship, so we thought the human identifying himself as Doctor Mercedes was in charge."

"He didn't explain our situation, and why he wasn't in hibernation?"

"We eventually determined your circumstances, but we could only deal with him. We explained that your ship shouldn't continue to our planet, and we outlined a plan to accomplish that objective. He was very cooperative."

"But you knew he wasn't the ship's Captain!" said Tina, her voice raised a bit in anger. "If you wanted to talk to me, I could have been awakened."

"Yes," replied Yeleng-Kan. "But after meeting Doctor Mercedes, we decided on a more efficient plan."

"Involving brainwashing and mutiny," said Tina, still registering annoyance.

Captain Yeleng-Kan paused, possibly trying to absorb the meaning of "brainwashing and mutiny." When he replied, he seemed almost apologetic.

"It seemed the easiest method of completing our assigned mission."

"Well, what about our mission, Captain?" asked Tina. "Did you ever consider the importance our planet has given to our voyage? Many of Earth's resources were purposefully diverted to a journey to your planet, as I assume you know."

"Yes, we're well aware of the history of your proposed voyage. However, you're not aware of the problems that could develop from visiting our world. Have you ever noticed, in your own planet's history, how discovery of new societies always seem to lead to disaster. Shall I remind you of the Europeans and the New World in the Americas?"

"Your knowledge of Earth's history is fascinating, Captain. But I'm afraid it doesn't explain why you would use devious methods to try to turn our ship around. We've adequately considered the consequences of visiting another planet — we've actually done it many times in history?"

"And what were those consequences, Captain Brett?"

Yeleng-Kan paused, seemingly purposefully, to let the question sink in. His strategy worked as intended, causing Tina to change her tone to one of compromise rather than irritation.

"Yes, we've experienced difficulty with colonial ambitions in space, but different from those of the original Europeans in the Americas. Our space missions have apparently not survived for long, based on our loss of communication with the colonists. What is there on your planet that's so important for us to avoid?"

"The cultural differences are extreme," replied Yeleng-Kan in what seemed a conciliatory tone. "We're over a 100 million years more advanced than humans, not just in technology but in all aspects of society. It would be a major blow for your world to encounter our civilization at this time."

"But we're doing fine at this conference table, aren't we?" countered Tina. "As I see it, this is the beginning of an opportunity for both of our worlds to learn from each other."

"Those are admirable thoughts, Captain Brett, but I'm afraid you don't understand how adversely affected your society would be by intricate contact with us. What you would take back to your planet could be disastrous."

"Are you referring to disease? Surely, we both have enough advanced technology to prevent it, after all these years."

"Actually, even disease is of concern, but it's not the greatest of the problems. Remember, you're the inferior culture this time. It's not like all of those previous instances on your planet when a more advanced society discovered a culture they considered less civilized and less developed. Believe me, it's best to just move on as an emerging galactic civilization as if you'd never met us."

"So wise. So humble," said Tina, again sounding irritated. "You've been watching Earth for centuries, haven't you? And you think you know us so well you can just come aboard our ship and tell us what to do."

"Captain Brett, we've been watching you for a lot longer than centuries. And more than just observing you."

"You've visited Earth?" asked Tina, incredulous that such a thing could happen without any evidence on Earth.

"Once, so long ago that there was no one to talk to. Devon-Chi, please assist me here," said Yeleng-Kan, turning towards the even shorter alien standing behind him. The smaller version of him – same tunic, same crew-cut, similar facial features – stood behind Yeleng-Kan, facing the three humans. "This is Devon-Chi, our philoso-historian, who can explain about our one and only visit to your planet."

Devon-Chi wasn't only smaller; she possessed softer facial features, and was less authoritarian looking, almost timid in appearance.

"It was during the era of the large animals you call dinosaurs," said Devon-Chi, a soft female voice that soothed the mood in the room but shocked the humans. At that instant, the three Earthlings suddenly realized Devon-Chi was a woman. She paused, watching their reaction, probably assuming their look of astonishment was that her planet's contact with Earth was so long ago. Which was true, but part of their startled reaction was the realization she was a woman.

"We've built galactic spaceships for a long time, but our visit to Earth – which we call 'LifeZone' – was before we had advanced surveillance technology. We knew there was life on your planet, but didn't know what we might find. These huge animals were an interesting discovery, unlike anything on our planet, even in it's distant history."

Tina, Cougar, and Tim listened intently. As Tina studied Devon-Chi, she decided the alien was beautiful in her own way, once the crew-cut image was set aside. She noticed her small breasts pushing against her tight gray tunic, sensual in appearance. Cougar, on the other hand, felt an instant surge of distrust for the woman, and then reassured herself it was probably because she had assumed the alien was a male, which somehow seemed deceptive. Tim seemed unable to focus on what Devon-Chi was saying, considering how overwhelmed he was by the day's events.

"These enormous animals were healthy and well adapted to their environment," continued Devon-Chi. "Our initial reaction was they could evolve into an intelligent society, given enough time to do so. What we didn't know is we were preparing them for their demise."

"They were eventually exterminated by climatic change," said Tina. "A dramatic alteration to their environment precipitated by Earth's collision with an asteroid or a comet."

"No," said Devon-Chi, softly as before, but with a tone of assertiveness. "It was us, not another object."

The three humans stared at Devon-Chi, waiting for her to clarify why she seemed so determined.

"We brought disease, although at the time we believed such contagion couldn't be transmitted across such distant genetic lines. In fact, we didn't even realize it could be spread from our society to any alien creatures on another planet. How wrong we were."

Devon-Chi sounded guilt-ridden, although the event had occurred 65 million years before her birth. Her feminine concern and soft demeanor showed through, as she focused her sad eyes on Tina.

"It was one of our planet's few brushes with alien life," said Yeleng-Kan, reaching back with his lower arm to rest his hand on the waist of Devon-Chi, as if to console her. "We were inexperienced, although there's no excuse."

These creatures were very much like humans, with similar emotions and a sense of compassion. They still felt guilt for something done by their forefathers millions of years ago.

"Disease, although a legitimate concern, isn't the primary obstacle today," said Yeleng-Kan. "Devon-Chi can explain further details about our disastrous voyage to LifeZone – let her tell you more when there's time – including how we damaged our own society by that early visit. No one benefits when vastly different cultures meet for the first time. In the case of LifeZone – sorry, Earth – it's way too early for you to make contact with us."

"But we've already made contact," said Tina. "We're sitting across from each other right now."

"But we're only a few individuals, and the rest of our societies are not involved," replied Yeleng-Kan. "Plus this is outer space, a vastly lower risk environment than a planet when it comes to the spread of disease. We're isolated here, both in terms of physical contact and societal implications. I know your intentions are good, but so were ours when we killed your dinosaurs. It's a miracle all of your planet's life wasn't exterminated by us. Our enviro-scientists say the incident would have been much worse were it not for the coincidence of the asteroid impact that came soon thereafter; destroying most of the disease agents we brought inadvertently to your planet. Our first contact could have prevented the development of humans."

"Since then, you watched human life evolve?" asked Tina.

Yeleng-Kan nodded, half-turned towards Devon-Chi, who smiled – a pretty smile – as he explained the details.

"We didn't have planetary surveillance technology at the time of our visit. But it became a significant tool in our search for alien intelligence in later years. By the time the first humanoids were developing, we were able to monitor their progress. Once you developed radio and television, everything became even easier. When the *Challenger* project began to evolve, we were able to follow it in detail. *Gardenpeace* was launched twenty years before your spaceship departed Earth, so we could intercept *Challenger* prior to its point-of-no-return."

"Do you use Thomson-Jump technology and cryogenic hibernation?" asked Cougar, speaking for the first time since the aliens entered the bridge.

"Jumps, yes. Cryogenics, no. Our jumps are bigger than yours, virtually unlimited in span. It took a single jump to get here from our planet. So we don't need cryogenic technology, although we used it in earlier eras."

"And you've visited other worlds than Earth, met other alien intelligences?" asked Cougar.

"We've searched almost all the way across the galaxy," replied Yeleng-Kan. "We've found many worlds with indigenous species, but none of them with alien intelligence like ours or yours."

"How sad," said Tina. "We've believed there were lots of alien worlds with intelligent beings. And we also believed their physical appearance would be totally unlike us."

"See – there's an example," said Yeleng-Kan. "In an instant you know the answer to one of life's greatest mysteries, and now you could return that knowledge to Earth with dire results. Something very unusual must have occurred in our obscure spiral arm, but it didn't happen elsewhere. It's no coincidence we look alike. Do you think that knowledge will contribute to your society?"

"Maybe not in a positive way," admitted Tina. "It's... Well, as I said, it's sad. But avoiding the truth is never a plausible scientific approach."

"There are only two planets where intelligent life evolved, based on what we've found so far," said Yeleng-Kan. "It would be best if your planet didn't know these details yet. When you're further advanced, come pay us a visit, and things may work out better. Not knowing can be one of the greatest driving forces in life."

"Such as the fact that we both speak English," said Tina, looking directly into Yeleng-Kan's eyes.

At first Yeleng-Kan tilted his head to the side, looking confused.

"Oh, a joke. I get it now," said Yeleng-Kan impassively.

They all laughed now, even the aliens standing behind the table.

"It's a remarkable accomplishment on your part," said Tina. "Learning what must be an entirely unique language so perfectly."

"For us, it's nothing," replied Yeleng-Kan. "Would you like to hear our own language?"

"Sure," replied Tina.

Yeleng-Kan pivoted his head around towards Devon-Chi, nodding as if saying: "Yes." She immediately demonstrated a soft murmur, more of a faint wavering tone than words as humans knew them. As she talked, her skin tone changed, noticeable in her hands and face, brightening as the inflection in her voice rose. The rhythm was smooth, a complete coordination of sound and body language. Her lower arms undulated gently as she talked.

When she stopped, Yeleng-Kan replied to her with a short murmur, and then changed promptly to English: "Devon-Chi explained to me the history of your original space exploration efforts, from your first orbiting satellites until the initial landing on your moon, quite an exciting period for the people of your planet."

"All that in just a few seconds!" exclaimed Tina, incredulous at the power of their language.

"Yes, another illustration for you to consider. You will eventually acquire such abilities with the aid of computers, but it may take millions of years. Your culture isn't ready for contact yet, unless you want it to end in disaster."

"So, if I hear you right, you're worried about Earth, even comparing it to an era like the extinction of the dinosaurs," said Tina. "Or are you afraid for your own sake."

"A little of both," replied Yeleng-Kan. "But mostly it's because you would be so adversely affected, being the less-advanced society. I remind you again of the Europeans and the American Indians, a grave example. The disease aspect could be similar, but it's more of a historic illustration than a valid concern. We have the medical technology to avoid the spread of contagion, and we can send you on your way without any real fears of physical harm. Our planet – Poseidon, as you call it – cares enough about the inhabited universe to want to help save you from yourself. So turn around now, and be done with it."

Yeleng-Kan ended abruptly, as if his statement was the end of the discussion, and there were no other possibilities.

"And if we don't, you'll blow us to smithereens," said Tina.

Yeleng-Kan glanced back at Devon-Chi, apparently trying to absorb the meaning, and then revealed a very human-like laugh. Now looking across the table at the three humans, he was smiling with his human-like mouth.

"No, you don't understand us very well," said Yeleng-Kan. "That's why the route we took with Doctor Mercedes seemed so reasonable. He would have turned you around without us having to intervene any further. And no one would have been hurt. One thing your society will learn as it grows older is that there is no long-term survival for those involved in the killing of others. I'm simply telling you not to continue to our planet. As they say on your world, a word to the wise is sufficient."

"You must not know as much about us as you assume," replied Tina. "Because there's another saying on Earth – it goes something like this: 'Trust in yourself.'"

"And you trust in yourself enough to go on, after all we've tried to explain to you? Please consider what's best for your own planet, Captain Brett."

"I'll do that, I promise," replied Tina. "And I'll talk it over with the rest of my crew. But what happens if we decide to get underway once again, with a Thomson-Jump directly towards Poseidon?"

"In that case, Captain Brett, *Gardenpeace* will back far away, and we'll say: 'Be careful, for you have made an ill-fated decision.' And then we'll wish you the best of luck."

## Chapter 20

## Beyond the Realm of Earth

"Devon-Chi was kind of cute, don't you think?" chided Tina.

"The length of our mission is starting to set in," said Cougar. "Now you're giving an alien a close look. It's enough to make me jealous."

"Don't I wish," replied Tina, sounding half-serious.

"Well, I really can't believe it," said Cougar. "Here we are in the middle of outer space, riding formation with an alien rocketship, and you're talking about doing it with the first female alien we've ever met."

"The first female alien anyone has ever met," added Tina.

"Well, since you brought it up – sex that is – what would you say if I told you I'm attracted to Tim?"

"Tim, the only guy still awake on the whole ship? The only guy for a ship full of women?"

"When you say 'full,' I assume you're talking quality rather than quantity," replied Cougar.

"You're seriously talking about Tim? Maybe your Captain's got her eye on him."

"Does she?"

"No."

"I'm just being theoretical here, Tina. What would be your reaction if I made a move on him?"

"My reaction would be that it's about time. He's been giving you that look for quite a while."

"What look? He hasn't paid the slightest bit of attention to me."

"Oh, really? Well, he sure seems to like spending time with you."

"That's only because I'm the only person he can talk to, other than his Captain. And Tim's no better about talking to his Captain than he was when he was a sergeant. Great respect for authority, I might add."

"I've noticed. Just like I've noticed him eye-balling you."

"Okay, okay. New subject. While you're ogling Miss Alien, and I'm chasing Mr. Sergeant turned Lieutenant, we probably have a few more pressing issues."

"True," said Tina. "Like getting our act together on the Thomson-Jump, if we're gonna' do it, that is."

"The three of us have already decided, haven't we?"

"Yes. We're going to do it, unless someone has changed their mind."

"I'm ready to continue with the checklist. Over half of it was finished when we shut things down for the rendezvous with *Gardenpeace*. I'm not sure we have to start at the beginning again. Can't we proceed from where we left off?"

"Per the flight manual, we can skip to Section Thirteen, which means we'll only need to repeat a few items," said Tina. "The environmental systems were disrupted by the alien boarding, so we'll reaccomplish that part of the Section Twelve checklist, and then continue from there. If we get started this afternoon, we'll be ready for the jump in four days, five max."

"Any special procedures for the cryo-cubes?" asked Cougar. "I doubt the flight manual has anything to say about it, since we always jump with all personnel awake."

"No, there's nothing in the manual, but it stands to reason there should be no ill effect on the cubes, any more than we're affected on the flight deck."

"What about the electrical flicker. Interruptions to the cryogenics process could be fatal, if the power disruption lasts very long."

"Well, we're not taking any chances by letting them out for a Thomson-Jump," said Tina. "I hate to sound so crude, but they'll just have to take whatever happens. I'm not risking anything when it comes to Mercedes and his gang of misfits."

"Understood. Jumping with cubes active is an acceptable risk."

"I've asked Tim to troubleshoot the low pressure we detected in the air-turbine-motor. The ATM doesn't come into play during a Thomson-Jump, but we'll need it on the other side, once we start to accelerate again."

"Probably nothing we can do about it now anyway," said Cougar. "It's a fly-until-fail item, designed to last almost indefinitely. If the pressure drops off further, we could try making a new one in the Fabricator."

"We'd need an EVA to replace it," said Tina. "Could do it in conjunction with the next garbage evacuation. Maybe we should replace it, even if the pressure doesn't decrease again. Losing an ATM in a critical phase of flight isn't worth the chance."

"Still, you're talking about after the Thomson-Jump, eh?"

"Right. We're busy enough as it is. And we're about to get a whole lot busier."

\* \* \* \* \*

When Cougar came off duty, Tina was already in bed, the night-light illuminating the path to the bunks. She didn't want to disturb Tina, so she undressed quietly and started to climb up into her bunk, pausing for a few seconds on the ladder.

Looking down at Tina, lying on her side and snuggled up to her pillow, Cougar thought for just a moment what it would be like to crawl in bed with her, and cuddle up close. There was no doubt Tina would be thrilled with such a decision, but so far Cougar had always cast the thoughts away as soon as they appeared. Tonight she paused, gave it one more thought, and then climbed the rest of the way to her upper bunk. She snuggled up to her own pillow, and fell asleep thinking about Tim.

\* \* \* \* \*

This was getting ridiculous. When her attention should be tuned to the upcoming Thomson-Jump, Cougar found herself lusting over Tim. Maybe it was true that the length of the mission was getting to the point where she actually needed male companionship, which would make it the first time in her life this was the case. She liked men, but she really didn't need them, or so she thought. If she discussed it with Tim, the whole subject might be resolved, or the topic could at least be brought out into the open. After the Thomson-Jump, they'd have more time for social interaction. The best thing, in Cougar's rationalizing mind, was to sit down with Tim, discuss it, and then move on.

When she saw him in the dining area, she didn't hesitate to take advantage of the situation. Grabbing a cup of coffee, she plopped down next to him at the table.

"Any luck with the ATM?" she asked.

"Not much I can do for it now, except run through the troubleshooting diagrams. The Captain thinks we should replace it, but I'm not sure I have much faith in the Fabricator."

"That's why we brought it along."

"I know," replied Tim. "But we've only used it for routine shipboard items, never for making a big component."

"It's designed for such a task. I think it'll handle an ATM just fine."

"Maybe," said Tim.

"You know, I wanted to ask you something, if you don't mind."

"Sure. What's up, Coug?"

It was a good start. He hardly ever called her "Coug," which was just too informal for a guy so by-the-book.

"You know we're both officers now, so some of the rules have changed."

Tim looked at her inquisitively, as if he didn't know what she was referring to, but she knew he must. Fraternization between enlisted members and officers was a technicality. Everyone knew it was forbidden, but not many had been arrested, especially in outer space. In the old days on Earth, men and women had fallen in love in the military, only to be tossed out of the service for crossing that boundary. The old days were gone, but the rules were still in the books.

"What rules?" asked Tim, as if a dimwit (which he certainly wasn't).

Nothing like making it tough for me, thought Cougar.

"Fraternization," she said.

"Oh," he replied, and said no more.

"Well, do you remember when we were kidding during your enlisted days, and you said: 'Too bad you're a lieutenant.'"

"Sure, I remember."

If it could go any slower, Cougar didn't know how.

"Well, when I said: 'Too bad you're a sergeant, Sarge,' I meant it."

"I meant it too. Sort of."

"Sort of? Look, Tim, what I'm trying to say is that I like you, and I thought we might get together more after the Thomson-Jump, when we have some time."

"Look, Cougar, I like you, too."

But no more "Coug." She felt embarrassed, and increasingly uncomfortable.

"Sorry, I didn't mean to bring it up," stammered Cougar.

"No, that's okay, Coug. I hear you, and I do like you. But you need to know something."

"Okay, Tim. What?"

"Well, I'm gay, and I thought you knew."

"Gay? I thought Kenny Childers was gay, but not you."

"Don't I wish Kenny was gay," replied Tim. "Heaven knows I tried, but he's as straight as they come."

"Oh."

Cougar chuckled to herself. Tim was gay, and Kenny Childers wasn't. So was Tina – more accurately, she was bi-sexual. Cougar was the only awake heterosexual human within 35 light-years.

At least now she could get back to her work, able to laugh at herself again.

\* \* \* \* \*

CHALLENGER HAD NOT TRANSMITTED an update to Earth since completion of the first Thomson-Jump. That message had been a routine report of their on-schedule mission progress. A lot had happened since then, including their discovery of the deceleration, the disturbing images from the onboard cameras, a near-mutiny, and contact with aliens. Tina knew this all should have been reported, but she had held off for reasons that weren't clear in her own mind. When Cougar had asked Tina whether she should transmit a report about the donut error and the discovery of the deceleration, Tina simply said: "Not yet. I'll let you know." Cougar, in her typical acceptance of whatever the Captain decided, replied with a nod of her head: "Okay, boss," she said.

Like a little white lie grown out of proportion, the lack of any subsequent reports from *Challenger* was far outside the mission rules. Tina knew it, Cougar knew it, and now it seemed too late to change.

"After our next jump, we'll send a complete update back to Earth," said Tina, and Cougar nodded.

But both of them knew they had fallen into a self-imposed trap. Maybe this was how it had begun when the colonialists reached outward beyond the effective grasp of Earth. For *Challenger*, the round-trip communication delay to home was already 70 years. It seemed so unimportant, like putting a message in a bottle, never expecting anything to come of it. When it came time to return to Earth, they'd need to think it all through. They'd have plenty of time to work things out.

Meanwhile, with *Gardenpeace* floating nearby, all three *Challenger* crewmembers were busy with their pre-jump duties, Cougar and Tina concentrating on the checklists, and Tim finishing his ATM troubleshooting and moving back to the training Tina had assigned him from the systems manuals.

The aliens had moved back aboard *Gardenpeace*, pulling slowly away from their position beside *Challenger*, to float about a kilometer away. When the aliens were finally ready to depart, it was a female's voice on the radio, definitely that of Devon-Chi. Tina preferred to think of the encounter from the standpoint that a lot had been accomplished between the two societies already – at least now that the aliens seemed to treat the humans with more respect. And she hoped their final communication with them would be pleasant. Maybe that's why Devon-Chi had been assigned the microphone.

"*Challenger*, this is *Gardenpeace*, with information regarding our departure from this sector of space," said Devon-Chi

"Go ahead, *Gardenpeace*," radioed Cougar from her position in the bow.

"When you're ready, we'll back off farther to your side, and then accelerate ahead when well clear. Captain Yeleng-Kan bids you farewell, and we all wish you a safe passage."

After their meeting on *Challenger's* bridge, there had been further discussion regarding what Tina and her crew should do. The representatives from both planets seemed to have reached an implied understanding that *Challenger* probably would move on to it's next Thomson-Jump in the direction of Poseidon. This brief radio exchange was the first since Yeleng-Kan's final arguments against such a decision. Tina felt she needed to say something more, so she broke into Cougar's communications link.

"*Gardenpeace*, this is Captain Brett. We appreciate your concern regarding our voyage to your planet, but we look forward to seeing you there."

"Roger, *Challenger*," replied Devon-Chi. "On behalf of Captain Yeleng-Kan, I wish you Godspeed. *Gardenpeace* will remain in the vicinity, pending your space jump. Let us know if we can be of any assistance."

Like two ships of the same space force, the giant gray shell of *Gardenpeace* moved away from *Challenger*, positioned briefly so the humans could see the ship's entire long slender outline as it slowly revolved around them. Then *Gardenpeace* darted forward at a tremendous pace, with no signs of propulsive jets being activated. In less than a minute it was a small grey speck against the black background, and then it was gone.

"On the edge of our radar coverage," announced Cougar. "Now it's disappeared. Must be accelerating at least a tenth of SOL already. Wow!"

"Like I said," replied Tina. "It's magic."

## Chapter 21

## EVA

"Environmental systems," said Cougar, running through the final portion of their checklist.

"Minimized. Scrubbers on standby," replied Tina.

When they reached the item for which their action was pretty much a guess, Tina deferred to Tim, who sat in front of her.

"Tim, during our first jump, I locked the hydraulic ATM in standby at this point. But I could leave it in override."

"I'd go with standby," he replied. "Pressure recovery should work best that way."

"Thanks," replied Tina. "Cougar, I'm setting hydraulics to standby."

"Very good, Captain. ATM in standby."

They completed their checklist, and then Tina added: "Anybody got anything else?" Which was her way of saying they were ready to go.

"Nothing to add," said Tim when Cougar didn't speak up immediately.

"Nada, Madam Captain," said Cougar. "Just another routine day in our little chunk of outer space."

"I certainly hope so," replied Tina.

She paused a few more seconds, and then reached forward to touch the screen command: "Activating Jump," she said. "Here's hoping Professor Einstein is still on duty."

Nothing happened, which was totally normal. The three of them sat there, pondering the situation calmly, Cougar pulling her reading slate from the side of her screen to pore over whatever trash novel she was in the middle of reading. It could be a long wait.

But it wasn't. After only a half-hour, the bridge lights started to blink, and they were gone.

\* \* \* \* \*

"Post-Jump checklist, when you're able," said Tina, as soon as the blinking lights turned steady again and her workstation computer flashed its reboot message.

"Waiting on my computer, Captain," replied Cougar calmly. "Checklist is now loading."

"ATM is fluctuating below six thousand PSI," announced Tim. "Now holding – no, still fluctuating – at fifty-five hundred, bottom of the green arc."

"Keep me posted, Lieutenant Halmer," said Tina, without any inflection in her voice that indicated concern. "What do you think about override?"

"Negative, Captain. Recommend remaining in standby for now. Pressure is steadying, increasing slowly. Looks stable at fifty-eight hundred for the moment."

"Okay, let me know before you switch to the normal setting."

"Roger, Captain. We should let it settle down a bit first."

"Post-Jump checklist is now available, Captain," announced Cougar.

"Okay, folks, let's get to it," replied Tina.

"Verification of Jump status," said Cougar.

"Jump verified as complete," announced Tina. "The only anomaly so far is the ATM pressure, which seems to be restoring itself. Continue."

"Personnel status," said Cougar.

"All is well," said Tina. "Tim, as soon as the ATM is switched back to normal, make a physical check of the active cryo-chambers. From here, the room images seem normal, and the cryogenics monitors indicate all three cubes are fully functioning."

"Roger, Captain."

"Systems condition," said Cougar.

"All systems except ATM are normal," stated Tina. "Tim, are you ready to switch out of standby mode?"

"Ready, Captain. The ATM has stabilized at six thousand PSI. Recommend switching to normal."

"Approved," said Tina curtly. "ATM set to normal."

"ATM to normal," repeated Tim. "It's looking good in that condition."

"Continue to monitor it for a few minutes, and then check the cubes," said Tina.

"Roger, Captain. Will comply."

Which he always did, not matter what he was asked to do. And Cougar, in her sometimes-slovenly way, was the same. No Captain could ask for more.

"Coug, put the checklist into pause mode, and give me a position report, please."

"Checklist is now in pause. Checking position… Right in the center of the donut!"

In a flash of time, their ship had moved 33 light-years closer to Poseidon. They were now prominently poised on the far side of their point-of-no-return.

"Continue the checklist," said Tina as if on autopilot, which she pretty much was.

Cougar began running through the routine items, now far enough down the checklist to know everything was safe after their leap across the galactic sea. It would take another half-hour to complete all of the items, but these were mostly routine verifications of what they already knew. The ship was, for the time being, out of harm's way on the other side.

"ATM is still stable in normal mode. Pressure is steady at six thousand PSI," said Tim. "Leaving the bridge to check the cubes."

"Thanks, Tim," said Tina. "Give me a call from there."

"Roger, Captain."

Militarily precise, when needed, and informally friendly when appropriate – Tina was proud of her little crew. It was a momentous occasion, for now they were committed to their destination, a planet where the smartest minds in the known universe predicted that their small contingent of spacefaring humans might destroy all the progress made on Earth since the species emerged from the savannahs of Africa. Quite a responsibility.

Tina slumped back in her seat for a moment, contemplating their situation before continuing the checklist.

"We're on our way again," said Tina out loud to no one in particular.

"Wouldn't have it any other way," replied Cougar.

\* \* \* \* \*

With their flight plan now pretty much back on schedule, *Challenger* accelerated to its maximum continuous speed of 0.13 SOL, with artificial gravity provided by the slow rotation of the ship around its axis. The bow shutters were closed again, making the view less disorienting by hiding the rotating sky. They were 68 light-years from Earth, 33 light-years to Poseidon, with eight months until their next hibernation period. That would be followed by the final Thomson-Jump almost into Poseidon's stellar system, but far enough outside to assure they didn't hit anything near their destination. Comet-like objects in their own solar system's Oort cloud extended far beyond the planets, and they expected it to be the same near this stellar system.

*Gardenpeace* was now well separated from *Challenger*; probably already home, if that's where they were headed next. Tina hadn't inquired regarding *Gardenpeace's* plans, and Captain Yeleng-Kan hadn't volunteered the information. When *Gardenpeace* rocketed away – "rocketing" akin to magic – both ships seemed to have accepted what was to come. The two crews hadn't reached a mutual agreement, but they'd parted in peace.

This in-between period, leading to the next cryogenic session, was a time for winding down after the hectic pace – a near-mutiny, followed by an alien encounter, and a jump of 33-light years. The ship's systems had to be monitored for the next eight months leading up to the final sleep session, but there was little more to do now.

After eleven days of routine operations since their recent Thomson-Jump, the air-turbine-motor suddenly showed increased signs it could no longer maintain its specified pressure. The ATM was one of three hydraulic motors on the ship. Two of the motors, which were performing flawlessly, used engine-driven drives, turbine-geared into the fusion thrust chamber. The ATM was only essential during initial acceleration, or during the final stages of deceleration, when the engine-driven hydraulic motors were abruptly changing speeds. Air to power the ATM was bled off the environmental system – air that would otherwise be recirculated – so the ATM only delayed the use of this extra flow. It wasn't a perpetual motion machine, but was as close as it gets. Their ship relied on the ATM during brief but critical maneuvers, like their upcoming entry into orbit around Poseidon.

It was a straightforward design – basically an air-driven turbine rotating a simple hydraulic motor. Their ATM was one of the few components with moving parts that was considered indispensable for their mission. Basically, there was only one moving module – a fan and its shaft connected directly to the hydraulic motor. True enough, a constant-speed-drive was also part of the package, but it too was of the simplest design. There was no backup, not through design deficiency, but because the mean-time-between-failure of this component was so large that no spaceship had ever experienced such a malfunction. The computed MTBF of the combined ATM and CSD was 14,000 years.

Other components on the ship were without backup for similar reasons, particularly since it would be impossible to carry enough spare parts to cover all of the contingencies. With the only warehouse located many light-years away, the best solution was to build-your-own whenever you needed new components. That's where the Bernardo Fabricator came in.

The crew had already turned to the Fabricator for a few routine items, although Tina nixed a number of replacements that would have been easy to construct. The Bernardo Fabricator was simply too important to their mission when it came to emergency repairs. To risk it for the construction of less-than-essential components might mean less chance of the Fabricator working properly when it was truly needed. So far, there had been three items constructed using the device – a fusion drive TD Amp (a temperature datum amplifier), an emergency hatch locking mechanism, and a replacement coffeemaker (which Tina didn't document in the ship's log). Several other items they didn't replace were considered too nonessential to make the grade for the Captain's approval. Still, life aboard *Challenger* remained lacking in almost no significant way. The ship's systems continued to operate flawlessly, and personnel comfort items were in top shape.

So when a replacement ATM was under consideration, the decision was simple. This component was crucial for their orbital insertion at Poseidon, and the time to replace it was now. Besides the need for the air-turbine-motor during acceleration and deceleration, the ATM served as an essential backup to the engine-driven hydraulic pumps during cryo-sessions, when it would automatically take over if needed while the crew was asleep.

An extra-vehicular activity session would be necessary to replace the ATM, but the crew was used to EVA's. They had conducted three of them so far, two for scheduled inspections of the exterior of the ship, and one to replace the faulty emergency hatch locking mechanism. All of the EVA's had included a opportunity for manual ejection of their onboard trash (safer than auto-ejection, which could damage the hull). Each of the previous EVA's was conducted by Major Lin and Sergeant Childers, since they were the systems experts.

All members of the crew except Doctor Mercedes and Tim Halmer (the medical portion of the crew) were trained in EVA. However, the ship's Captain was forbidden by regulations (except during an emergency) to leave the spaceship while it was underway, and the NavCom seldom had a reason to conduct an EVA.

"I could go out with Cougar," said Tina, when meeting with her crew to discuss the plan to replace the ATM. "Regulations forbid it, of course, but we're an awfully long way from Earth for anybody to complain."

"They'd probably call back after the hundred-plus years of communication lag, and say you shouldn't have done it, eh?" joked Cougar.

"I'd be glad to go with Cougar," said Tim. "After floating around in here during our weightless periods, it can't be much different."

"Except, don't forget to hang on to your tether," said Tina. "That's how the Space Force loses a lot of lieutenants."

They all laughed over that. But in the end, Tina decided two people outside were essential for safety, and Cougar and Tim were the best choice. Tim's strength and obvious mechanical ability would be an asset when dealing with a component that had never been removed from the hull.

The Bernardo Fabricator was another area where they needed to be innovative. The only crewmembers trained on the device were Lin and Childers, again because it was part of the systems area of responsibility.

"I'm not about to wake one of them up to run the Fabricator," said Tina. "The last thing we need around here is a mutineer equipped with power tools."

Tina decided Tim would study the flight manual to learn how to operate the device. How hard could it be, since it was another of the ships semi-automated subsystems, basically an advanced tool of CAD-CAM (computer-aided-design and manufacture), using lasers to construct almost anything from raw materials. It was one of the closest things to "magic" that Earthlings had invented, and thus it was more a matter of watching it happen than making it happen.

Under Tim's meticulous attention, the Fabricator spit out a new ATM from the design specifications he entered from Kim Lin's workstation, with Kim's password retrieved by Tina from the ship's master computer. In the corner of the gymnasium where the Bernardo Fabricator was stored, lasers cut the raw materials (mostly titanium, some Kevlar, and a few substances none of them recognized). Under a shielded cover, the Fabricator buzzed along for 45 minutes. Then, just like that, a new ATM was born.

The next day, while they were planning out the EVA, a pleasant-sounding female voice boomed over the speakers. It was Devon-Chi.

"*Challenger*, this is *Gardenpeace*, listening on guard frequency."

"Go ahead, *Gardenpeace*," replied Cougar, as soon as she could don her headset.

"Just so you know, we haven't been following you, except to monitor your activity from the distance in case you need assistance. We've noticed your decrease in velocity and the decrease in longitudinal rotation. Are you experiencing any difficulties?"

Cougar turned to Tina, and saw the Captain holding up her hand: "Wait, let me reply," she seemed to be saying, as she picked up her headset.

"Hello, Devon-Chi, this is Captain Tina Brett. Thanks for your concern, but we need no assistance. Our longitudinal rotation and forward velocity have been slowed in preparation for extra-vehicular activity involving replacement of one of our ship's components and routine ejection of trash."

There was silence, longer than Tina would have expected for a reply. It lasted nearly a minute, while Tina puffed her lips in a cute pouty pose that Cougar interpreted as: What's going on here? Finally, Devon-Chi answered.

"*Challenger*, Captain Yeleng-Kan would like to advise that we would appreciate it if you would avoid ejecting trash from your spacecraft.

He has asked me to convey that he means this in a constructive way, since we're sure you too want to preserve our environment."

The next pause on the radio was at *Challenger's* end, where Tina let out a sigh, and then spoke over her crew's hot mike.

"Is he joking? Here we are – over thirty light-years from the nearest planet, and this guy is telling us not to toss our trash."

"Maybe we're like Lewis and Clark paddling down the Columbia River," joked Cougar. "Hey, Clark, dump that stuff in the water. Who'll ever know?"

"Roger, *Gardenpeace*, we copy," said Tina. "Tell your Captain we respect his concern. Our EVA will be for replacement of a hydraulic motor. No trash."

"Thanks, *Challenger*. Captain Yeleng-Kan sends his regards, and requests you advise us when your EVA is complete. And let us know if any assistance becomes necessary. We'll be standing by."

"All of a sudden, these are different people," said Tina over the crew's hot mike. "If you can call them 'people.' They seem to be genuinely worried about us. What a change in attitude."

"Not once have they threatened our safety," replied Cougar. "Then again, if we dump our trash, they might blow us out of the sky."

Tina was still giggling when she replied to Devon-Chi.

"*Gardenpeace*, *Challenger* will advise upon completion of our EVA. Thanks."

"*Gardenpeace*, out," said Devon-Chi.

To Cougar's fine-tuned ear and imagination, she thought Devon-Chi was smiling. \* \* \* \* \*

THE EVA WENT BASICALLY as planned, although Tim needed to wrench on the old ATM more than he expected in order to break it loose from its enclosure in the midsection of the crew module. Cougar hung onto Tim's feet, as his whole body started to rotate when he turned the fasteners. The tool specified for the removal and replacement (also built using the Bernardo Fabricator) worked as outlined in the systems manual, and they were back inside the ship after an EVA of 47 minutes. No trash was ejected, and Cougar noticed Tim held on to his tether with his free hand continually while outside, even when he was working on the ATM.

Once back inside the spacecraft, Tina waited for Tim to climb out of his spacesuit, and then asked if it was okay to turn on the new ATM.

"Make it go," said Tim. "But it might take a few seconds to come up to pressure. I'd expect it to cavitate a little before it properly pumps fluid."

She hit the switch. The ATM didn't cavitate, because it didn't even turn on. No pressure, no indicator light, nothing.

"Not good," said Tina. "Could the electrical relay be bad?"

"I'm not sure," said Tim. "We didn't touch the relay. Maybe something went wrong with the Fabricator. I'd say that's more likely than anything we did when replacing the ATM. It's a real simple slide-in rack, with no connections to mess with."

"We can go back out and reseat the unit," suggested Cougar. "But Tim's right. The removal and replacement was so straightforward that it seems nothing could be wrong with the placement of the ATM. I'd vote for the component itself being bad – our Fabricator ain't properly fabricating."

They looked at each other in silence. Tina tried activating the switch a few more times. The ATM still didn't operate.

"Maybe it's time to wake someone up," said Tina.

"Oh, good," replied Cougar. "A raging lunatic with a laser. Just what we need."

"Well, it might be our only alternative," said Tina. "According to the flight manual, the ATM must be activated during orbital entry. Without it, we could fly right on by without stopping. I'd say a lunatic with a laser is the lesser of the evils."

"Especially if we keep our stun guns handy," noted Tim.

"Let's think it through before taking any action," said Tina. "I'll let *Gardenpeace* know about our situation, and then we'll talk about who we'll wake up, if we awaken anyone at all."

## Chapter 22

## Hitchhikers

They agreed that awakening Sergeant Childers was the best solution. He was the hands-on systems mechanic, while Major Lin was the systems manager. What they needed right now was a mechanical expert. Besides, they all felt more comfortable about Kenny Childers, and they'd even questioned whether he was involved in the mutiny plot. Innocent or not, he seemed the best person to call on for assistance.

When Sergeant Kenny Childers awoke, he found himself looking at a gun pointed directly at him by Cougar, both hands on her outstretched pistol, with Tim standing next to her holding another gun pointed down towards the floor.

"I'd tell you not to make a move," said Cougar. "But I guess that's pretty obvious. Take your time to regain your balance. We aren't going anywhere for now."

Kenny Childers looked ill, but faces seldom looked cheerful when first awakened from cryo-sleep. He glanced over at Tim, and gasped.

"Now I've seen everything," said Childers, staring at Tim's brown bars. "Are you really an officer?"

"Yes," replied Tim. "Captain Brett gave me a field promotion. I doubt she'll do the same for you."

"Probably not, based on the last time I saw her," replied Kenny. "But I wasn't involved with Mercedes' plans. Major Lin tried to convince me to join them, but I didn't. Could I have something to drink?"

Cougar let one hand off her gun, and carefully handed Kenny a bottle of water she had tucked into her coveralls pocket.

"Thanks, Cougar. I guess you think I'm guilty, too."

"Doesn't matter. We only woke you up so you can help with a little systems problem we have. If you try anything in the meantime, it's right back into the freezer."

"Okay, okay. What's the problem?"

"The ATM was losing pressure," replied Tim. "So we built a new one with the Fabricator, and replaced it. Now it's completely inop – no pressure, no sign of activation at all."

"Have you tried reseating the pump in its tray?"

"Not yet. But on our EVA, I made sure it was pressed firmly into the rack. The access door closed tight, so I think that indicates the ATM is all the way into the tray."

"You're right, Tim… oh, Lieutenant I mean. If the door latches, the pump is properly seated. Sounds like a problem with the Fabricator."

"Is there any way to check that out?" asked Cougar, lowering her pistol towards the bottom of the cryo-bed where Kenny's feet dangled.

"Sure, I'll get right on it. Whatever you say. We can't go into orbit around Poseidon without the ATM. Shouldn't try another Thomson-Jump either."

"That's what the flight manual says," replied Cougar. "But what about keeping the main pumps running during our deceleration burn to keep the hydraulic pressure up?"

"Real chancy," said Kenny. "There's no constant-speed-drive on the engine-driven pumps, so they'll drop off the line. That's why we have an ATM in the first place. Besides, of course, as a backup source of hydraulics."

"We'd normally give you longer to recover," said Cougar. "But we just can't spend the extra time now."

"I understand," replied Kenny.

"Fix yourself something to eat in the dining area," said Cougar. "Tim, keep him covered while he eats. Then make sure he goes directly to the Fabricator."

\* \* \* \* \*

Sergeant Childers couldn't find anything wrong with the Fabricator, so Tina directed him to use it to construct another ATM. Then Cougar and Kenny would try another EVA to replace the problematic component a second time.

"As a reminder, Sergeant, it wouldn't be wise to do anything stupid once you're outside the ship," said Tina in her command voice.

"Of course not, Captain," replied Childers. "Although you do know that a stun-gun isn't designed to operate in a zero-pressure environment."

Tina didn't know why he would mention this, but maybe it was just to show off his knowledge of the weapon. Actually, she didn't know the gun wouldn't operate in space. Maybe he was trying to show her how valuable his skills were, trying to keep them from throwing him back in the freezer. In either case, Tina didn't plan to give him any slack.

"No problem, Kenny. Cougar doesn't need a gun out there. I can control your spacesuit environmentals from the bridge. If you start to gag, you can assume I've noticed you fucking up."

Kenny stared at her with an incredulous look. Then he saw her giggle, and his face loosened up a bit.

"You can count on me to do what I'm told," said Kenny.

"Look, just do what we tell you to do," said Tina. "We don't have any direct evidence you were in on a mutiny, and I'll admit that. But you sure were in the wrong place at the wrong time. So for now, with us trying to hold this mission together with duct tape, you're going back into cryo-sleep after we fix the ATM. I promise we'll give you a chance to prove yourself once we arrive at Poseidon."

Kenny didn't say anything to that, indicating he wasn't sure whether he could trust her to give him a fair trial. No one had brought him up to date regarding the existence of the aliens, and Tina didn't feel it was appropriate now. After a lengthy pregnant pause, he spoke up again, changing the subject.

"Did you take care of the trash during your EVA," asked Kenny, motioning towards Cougar and Tim.

"We don't do that any more," replied Tina, lifting her eyebrows and looking over at Cougar.

"You don't eject the trash manually any more?" asked Kenny, looking astonished.

"We don't do it manually. We don't do it with the remote arm. We don't do it at all. There's room to store it until we reach Poseidon."

"You're kidding!"

"No, Kenny, I'm not kidding. A lot has changed since we put you in the freezer."

\* \* \* \* \*

THE SECOND EVA WAS no more successful than the first. The newly fabricated ATM snapped perfectly into place, and the access door closed firmly against it. But when Tina flipped the switch, once again nothing happened.

They were out of ideas, and they were scheduled for another 5-year cryo-session, which Tina didn't want to attempt without a backup hydraulic system. Even if they somehow worked it out, the sleep period was to be followed by another Thomson-Jump, which involved deceleration followed by subsequent acceleration. If that weren't enough, they would then go into orbit around Poseidon, where they would prepare their shuttle for the trip down to the planet. Three major mission events required something they didn't have – an ATM.

\* \* \* \* \*

"*GARDENPEACE*, THIS IS *CHALLENGER*, OVER," said Cougar into the microphone.

"Go ahead *Challenger*. We're reading you loud and clear," replied Devon-Chi almost instantly.

"You've probably noticed we've been sitting here for a while, still working on our mechanical problem. It's a hydraulic motor, air-driven, and we've manufactured a new one – twice, in fact. But when we swap it out each time, the motor still fails to activate. It's a necessary backup to our basic hydraulic system, and essential for maneuvering. Basically, we're dead in the water."

"I don't think our manufacturing equipment will respond to your ship's specs," replied Devon-Chi. "We're set up for our own parts specifications, but not for yours. I'll check on it further, but I'm pretty sure that's the case. Is there any other way for us to be of assistance?"

"Roger, *Gardenpeace*, we understand. Our Captain is standing by to talk to Captain Yeleng-Kan."

"Go ahead, *Challenger*. Captain Yeleng-Kan is monitoring this frequency."

"Spaceship *Gardenpeace*, this is Captain Tina Brett of the spaceship *Challenger*, with a request."

"Go ahead with your request," replied Yeleng-Kan.

"Well here it is," said Tina. "Can we bum a ride?"

There was a brief pause, maybe one of translation, and then Yeleng-Kan laughed into the microphone. In the background was the wavering tone the aliens had demonstrated during their visit to *Challenger*.

"We'd be glad to give you a ride," said Yeleng-Kan. "It's a quick trip to Poseidon, and it happens to be where we're both headed."

* * * * *

THEY DIDN'T PUT KENNY CHILDERS back into his cryo-cube, but they watched him closely during the day, and tied his legs and wrists during the night. The other two frozen prisoners were slowly awakened, a process taking a full day to assure no damage was done to their bodies. Both Mercedes and Lin were kept heavily drugged and bound at their wrists and feet, since Tina didn't trust them in the least. By the time the two men were fully recovered from cryogenics effects, *Gardenpeace* was alongside, preparing to dock with them.

When the three-person boarding party stepped onto *Challenger's* bridge (Yeleng-Kan, Devon-Chi, and a third man Cougar thought she recognized from their previous visit), Tina's crew (minus Mercedes, Lin, and Childers) was there to greet them. Cougar noticed Devon-Chi's face seemed to turn red when she first glanced at Captain Tina Brett. In return, Tina seemed thrilled to see Devon-Chi, but then immediately turned her attention to Yeleng-Kan.

"We welcome you again to our ship," said Tina. "Please sit with us," she said, motioning to the conference table.

"We'll try to make it a bit more pleasant this time," said Yeleng-Kan, as all six of them found seats at the table, aliens on one side, humans on the other.

"As we say on Earth, live and learn," said Tina.

"That goes both ways, Captain," replied Yeleng-Kan.

Both sides had come a long way, and now they seemed to be on parallel paths. Although Tina, Cougar, and Tim hadn't discussed it directly, abandoning *Challenger* could be the end to their links with Earth. Supposedly the aliens' communication technology would allow faster-than-light transmissions. But they weren't going home. In their minds, it had always been a two-way voyage, and now that possibility seemed remote. Had it been something similar for the colonists previously sent out from Earth? Although they entered their colonial journeys with few chances of ever returning home, there might have been more to it than that, which was precisely what Tina wanted to discuss.

The aliens were all seated now, but they seemed anxious, the same quick movements of their lower arms that they used to establish their balance. They slowly settled down, and no one said anything for a few minutes until the aliens appeared more relaxed at the table. The silence seemed mutually agreed upon, an understanding across species lines.

"Captain Yeleng-Kan, I've been thinking about something I'd like to ask," said Tina finally, appearing apprehensive.

Yeleng-Kan pushed back in his seat, raised himself up from his chair with his lower arms, and spoke slowly.

"There's much we need to discuss. It's appropriate for both of us to open ourselves to each other."

"I agree, Captain. So let's begin here... In your society's expansion into space, have you visited any of our colonial worlds?"

"Of course, we've been almost everywhere within 500 light-years of our planet, even farther during occasional missions across the galaxy. We visited your colonial planets before your missions arrived, and then more frequently after your species settled down in their new homes."

"And you found no intelligent life on these planets?" asked Tina.

"Not unless you consider humans intelligent," chided Yeleng-Kan.

It was a joke, and it sank in almost immediately. First the three aliens laughed, and then it quickly spread across the table to the humans. Yes, they had come a long way, maybe best demonstrated by the blatant cross-species wisecrack.

"Sorry, I just had to say that," said Yeleng-Kan, when the murmurs settled down.

"I'm glad we can laugh together," smiled Tina. "But I think you know why I'm asking this. Did your confrontations with human colonists end favorably?"

"Well, the instances varied considerably. In some cases, the humans were struggling miserably with their new environments, and we were able to help, and then departed without any adverse consequences. In other cases, mostly where humans had established a firmer foothold, we were received as enemies, and we found it difficult to communicate properly."

"What you're politely trying to say is they were hostile, and refused to accept you," said Tina.

"Yes, Captain, that was often the case. If they were fully functioning as a colonial society and working their way forward, it was a much more confrontational situation. However, I'm proud to say we were always able to eventually calm the colonists and agree upon mutual goals before we left. There was an unfortunate event at Alpha Centauri where one human was killed, but it was an accident precipitated by one of our ship's captains who was trying to... persuade... a human political official of our peaceful intent."

"Which explains the nearly universal loss of communication between our colonies and Earth," said Tina. "They became convinced your home planet and ours should remain autonomous from each other."

"Well, it wasn't only that," said Yeleng-Kan. "There is also the matter of limitations on the speed of communications, which tends to reduce the desire of your colonies to communicate with Earth."

"But you possess the knowledge necessary to break that communication barrier."

"Yes, although we haven't shared that technology with any of your colonies. That's been our choice, and we feel it's the right one."

"Because you think it's too early for Earth to know you exist," stated Tina.

"That's true," said Yeleng-Kan emphatically. "Once your planet makes the strides it's destined to make on its own soil, you'll be ready."

"Which means millions of years," replied Tina somewhat sarcastically.

"It can happen quickly, as it did with us," said Yeleng-Kan. "It could be thousands of years rather than millions."

"I suppose that means you won't help us communicate with Earth," replied Tina.

"If you decide to send a message back to Earth, we won't try to stop you, but we won't aid your actions by providing you with our faster-than-light method."

"Is there a possibility this decision will be changed when we reach your planet and talk to your leaders?" asked Tina, trying to sound less irritated than she really was.

"You need to understand how leadership is handled on our planet – which we call 'Garden,' by the way. We have a very flexible leadership structure, something we've developed over millions of years to allow our spaceships to operate efficiently light-years from home. Each ship's captain has complete decision authority without communication with Garden. Once these decisions are made, they're logged into the files of our leadership team at home. They would never attempt to change one of these judgments. So decisions flow smoothly, without being questioned by others within our command hierarchy."

"Now that's something that would take millions of years to achieve on Earth," laughed Tina.

"It has worked well for us," replied Yeleng-Kan. "In the case of our decisions regarding your colonies, it couldn't have been any other way. Each situation was different, and each of our captains had to take charge of the circumstances to resolve it properly."

"So you feel confident none of our colonies will attempt to contact Earth, and disclose you presence?" asked Tina.

"No, they present no risk to Earth's discovery of our society. Except for you, of course."

Which seemed to be the concern behind everything that had happened since *Challenger's* unexpected deceleration during their first cryo-session.

\* \* \* \* \*

WHEN THE CREW OF *CHALLENGER* moved aboard *Gardenpeace*, it was less dramatic than expected. The interior of the alien ship was much like their own, considerably larger but with rooms laid out in a similar format. The bridge was in the bulbous nose, as expected. There seemed to be enormous overkill when it came to the physical size of habitable areas, but apparently the ship's powerplant was nearly unlimited in thrust and endurance. The spaceship was 11 kilometers long.

*Gardenpeace* had a crew of 17, four officers, including Yeleng-Kan and Devon-Chi, while the rest were specialists referred to (at least in the English translation) as "stewards." The ship's bridge contained only three workstations, but the room's format was somewhat similar to *Challenger's*. The monitors were entirely three-dimensional in terms of projected images, and there were no other visible spacecraft controls. Apparently, there was even more automation than on *Challenger*, and the few necessary controls were embedded into the 3-D screens.

The dining area was at least five times the size of *Challenger's*, and it could be reconfigured quickly into a theater, meeting room, or a huge comfortable lounge. There were almost always some aliens active in this room, regardless of its configuration. The gymnasium, also considerably larger, was a popular area, with quick physical reformatting for a team sport resembling basketball and a game played on skate-like shoes that seemed similar to field hockey. As Tina said to Cougar when she first saw the huge gym: "That proves it – you can't call someone an 'alien' when their obvious love for sports is as intense as ours. It's like a common language unto itself."

The food was surprisingly appetizing. The automated dispensers provided a wide variety of vegetables that paralleled foods they were familiar with, such as lettuce, celery, and even a green knobby bud Cougar thought was a duplicate of brussel sprouts. They steered away from the meats and chicken-like offerings for now, not knowing how they would affect their digestive system, eating only the vegetables and grainy-looking breads. They ate well, and eventually expanded their menu to the unfamiliar items, most of which were delicious and none of them a digestive problem. It was another indication these two seemingly-divergent species had a lot in common.

When Tina and Cougar met together in the dining area, they often intentionally sat at tables with the aliens. None of them spoke perfect English (except Yeleng-Kan and Devon-Chi), but the interaction was fun, and they somehow managed to communicate beyond the language barrier. When they sat and ate with the aliens, they sometimes looked at these vigorous-looking individuals (mostly males), and thought about the healthy Europeans who brought deadly diseases to the New World.

\* \* \* \* \*

Two days after they moved into *Gardenpeace*, the ship began to move away from *Challenger*. Tina, Tim, and Cougar were invited to the bridge to watch the maneuver, although they had to stand at the rear of the room, since Yeleng-Kan and two other officers occupied the three workstations. The aliens talked among themselves in their own language, but mostly they sat quietly and watched their screens as *Gardenpeace* slipped rapidly away. There was no feeling of acceleration, and the ship wasn't rotating, as evidenced by the spectacular view through the see-through (from inside) bow. From here, the panorama was transparent in all directions except rearward, like a huge glass-enclosed cockpit. It was a melancholy moment for Tina and her small crew as the spaceship that had brought them 68 light-years across the galactic sea disappeared from view. They were now alone, without a vessel of their own, farther from home than any humans had ever traveled.

Within *Gardenpeace*, artificial gravity was somehow provided, although there was no rotation of the ship. Even as the visual cues indicated a rapid acceleration, they felt completely unaffected, while a steady force registered in their bodies, slightly less than 1-G. In a society so advanced that it's technological marvels seemed impossible, there was only one way to accept them – as magic.

*****

When Tina discussed what to do with their three prisoners, Yeleng-Kan asked for them to be turned over to him for security. Since it was his ship, it seemed only appropriate, although Tina feared what might happened if the aliens, who seemed overly tolerant in matters involving personal surveillance, provided Mercedes or Lin too much freedom.

Within a few days, Tina's fears were eased, when she saw Mercedes, Lin, and Childers moving around the ship freely. It seemed the last thing on their minds was to cause trouble. Lin and Childers were often seen together, which made sense considering their systems background. Mercedes always stayed by himself, occasionally eating with Lin, but never approaching any of the other humans, and staying away from the aliens. When Cougar or Tina saw Mercedes in a close setting within the ship, Mercedes always managed to maneuver out of the way, and that is the way they all preferred it.

Then, one day when Cougar entered the dining area for breakfast, she saw Mercedes sitting by himself at a four-person table. For a moment, she wanted to leave the room immediately, but then she changed her mind. She dispensed her breakfast of fruit (which looked exactly like strawberries, except they were orange), a yellow-green juice she liked, and a slice of grainy bread with a touch of a butter-like garnishment that seemed to have almost no flavor. Without hesitating, she walked over to Mercedes' table.

"Do you mind if I sit down?" she asked, looking down at the surprised doctor.

"Sure, sure, Cougar. Have a seat, please."

He actually rose as she sat down, an act of chivalry towards a lower-ranking female crewmember that was uncommon on any spacecraft in her illustrious career. If she hadn't felt so tense, she probably would have laughed.

"So, it looks like the Captain is giving you a lot more freedom than we offered," said Cougar, moving her bowl of fruit around as something to do.

"He's very accommodating," said Mercedes.

"Accommodating? That's pretty hard to do this far out in space."

"Coug, I'm not sure what you think happened to me, but there's more to it than you know."

"I bet there is. Go ahead, I'm listening."

Mercedes looked suddenly relieved. He reached across the table, about to lay his hand on her arm. Cougar snatched her hand back, dropping it into her lap below the table.

"Okay," said Mercedes. "I know you and Tina think I simply decided to turn on you for no reason. But it wasn't that way. During the deceleration, in the midst of the first cryogenics session..."

"The deceleration that you lied about!" interrupted Cougar, obviously hostile.

"Yes, I lied about it, but I had no choice. During the deceleration, this same alien ship forced their way aboard. Pirates. Very evil pirates, in fact."

He stopped, waiting for Cougar to absorb these facts. He looked confident.

"I know all about it," said Cougar matter-of-factly.

Dr. Donald Mercedes no longer looked confident. His eyebrows were raised when he spoke again.

"You knew? I guess that means they told you."

"They didn't need to tell us. We saw it all on the ship's cameras. There's two in almost every room, you know."

"You saw the aliens come aboard?" asked Mercedes, now looking pale.

"Yes, we saw them. And we also saw you in the cryogenics chamber during our second sleep session, injecting the drugs into Lin and Childers."

"They made me do it," said Mercedes. "The aliens brainwashed me somehow – I really don't know how they did it, but they made me inject the drugs, too."

"We know that, although we weren't sure about Kenny."

"Something went wrong with Kenny's cube. He was affected a little, but not like Lin. But if you know all about it, can't you look me in the eye and forgive me for something pirates forced me to do."

"I could, I suppose," replied Cougar. "But we saw the other tapes, too."

"You mean pictures? What others?"

"There's a record of you in the cryo-chamber, both sessions, including when you put me to sleep after my surgery. Tina reviewed those images thoroughly."

Mercedes looked suddenly ill. He coughed, and it looked like he was choking for a moment. Then he put his head down and shook it before looking up again. When Tina saw his eyes, they were glassy, almost crying.

"That's not all we saw," said Cougar. "I reviewed the tapes of the second cryo-session, including before you drugged Childers and Lin. When you checked Tina's cube as she fell asleep."

Mercedes nodded slowly. Then he pushed back from the table and started to stand. He raised himself up, looking wobbly.

"My head hurts," he said.

"Funny about that, isn't it? You're kind enough to give me a new brain, and you waste your old one."

"Sorry, I've got to go. I think I'm going to be sick," he said as he backed away from the table, turned and started walking to the door.

"I hope so," said Cougar, as he stepped away.

Chapter 23

**Garden**

Garden – what the Earth's astronomers referred to as Poseidon – loomed ever larger from the transparent bridge. Tina and Cougar stood, while Yeleng-Kan, Devon-Chi, and a small alien named Kelten-Iva sat at the three workstations. The Captain was in the rear seat, with Kelten-Iva at the front, where he seemed to be activating what few control actions were required.

As the Captain and Kelten-Iva took care of the ship, Devon-Chi walked back from her center seat to casually talk to Cougar and Tina, speaking low so she wouldn't distract the others from their jobs.

"There's really not much to do, but it's important for the Captain to have time to think, just in case something unusual happens. He always handles things that way, although problems almost never occur."

"That's an improvement our ships could use," commented Tina. "Time to think is important for any commander."

Kelten-Iva's job is a lot like yours, Cougar," noted Devon-Chi. "He has less actual control over the ship than you would, with an automated voice announcing key actions over his headset now and then. Here, I've put it through the translator so you can hear the first announcement," she said, handing frail-looking purple wireless headphones to Tina and Cougar.

They listened for a few seconds, until the expected broadcast arrived: "Trajectory normal, no action required," said a soft female voice.

"Princess!" said Cougar.

"Who?" asked Devon-Chi.

"Our automated voice on *Challenger* sounds almost exactly the same," said Tina. "Same calm by-the-book voice."

"Oh," laughed Devon-Chi. "We began using female voices in our countdown sequence millions of years ago. Psycho-specialists determined women's voices worked better in tense situations."

"Same for our ships," replied Tina. "But for us it was hundreds of years ago, which sounds puny compared to millions."

"Great minds think alike," replied Devon-Chi with a smile. "Our trajectory will bring us nearly directly to a spaceport near my home town. We'll fly an arcing path down to Garden rather than an orbital insertion like we used to do."

"Our ships can't slow down fast enough to make a direct landing," said Cougar. "So we enter stable orbits, and a shuttle take us down the rest of the way."

"More jobs for navigators," replied Devon-Chi. "Which isn't a bad thing."

They all laughed. It was much like interactions between human professionals everywhere. Obviously these aliens had developed in a similar way in this small region of space where the only known intelligent life in the universe resided. Had they, in fact, come from the very same seeds?

Tina's human crew would probably spend the rest of their lives on this planet with individuals they now referred to as aliens, but were they so different? Humans obviously weren't going to be able to exchange genes or interbreed, based on what they knew so far regarding the unusual (to them) sexual traits of these beings. But could they establish their own human generations here? Maybe the more important question was whether they felt it was necessary to do so. If they could live in the same environment as the aliens, and it looked like they would be able to that, could they learn to love another species?

"It's pretty startling," said Cougar, turning towards Tina. "We're going to plop down at a spaceport in less than an hour, cutting our way through an atmosphere similar to Earth's, heating up to who-knows-how-hot in the process. Maybe 'plopping down' isn't the best term."

"That's pretty much how we're going to do it," replied Devon-Chi. "The high temperatures will tear a layer off *Gardenpeace*, but she's designed to withstand it. You won't feel the heat in here, but you'll see it. The bridge is the best place to watch the show."

"What about the gravitational forces?" asked Tina. "Should we find a position to brace ourselves?"

"No, you can stand right here," said Devon-Chi. "Our ships are designed to absorb all forces as they occur, providing immediate feedback to our environmental absorbers. The absorbers actively reshape the interior structure, so you don't feel any of the movement."

"Amazing," said Tina. "Just standing here and watching a hell-fire re-entry."

And a hell-fire it was. When the heat developed, it spread around the ship in all directions, redder and redder, and then white-hot balls of flame piled around them on the transparent walls. There wasn't the slightest feeling of heat or vibration. In a few minutes, the glow returned to cherry red, and then was suddenly gone. Deep blue sky surrounded the ship, as they descended at what seemed an excessively steep angle, almost straight down.

The planet was composed of a single continent, surrounded by an all-encompassing ocean. It was an enormous island in the midst of a water world in all directions. The terrain was jagged, with tall mountains shrouded by green forests, interspersed with deep valleys teeming with rivers and lakes. From an altitude of about 30 kilometers, Cougar began to notice surface details indicating signs of intelligent life – narrow winding structures that might be roads or similar transportation arteries, as well as small regions carved out of the forests and river valleys where cities could lie.

There was the spaceport! The angle of descent was still steep, so the target in front of them seemed obvious. It included a series of lengthy paved areas at various angles, more rectangular than was the case with skinny, traditional runways on Earth. Tall skyscrapers were set back from the landing pads, seemingly encased in glass, reflecting brightly on their sunlit sides.

They were closing fast with the ground. About 10 kilometers up, the ship shifted quickly from its acute angle to a horizontal position as they descended more slowly to the ground. They came down, ever so gradually now, with the 11-kilometer long spaceship parallel to the surface during its final descent. They watched the ground rising below them, the transparent bow allowing them to see directly down. One dark rectangle at the center grew quickly larger, with angled lines and alphanumeric markings on the black pavement, a bulls-eye of sorts. Slowly they descended to the surface, with the world seeming to flatten out in all directions. Then everything stopped – they were down!

It took only a few minutes for Yeleng-Kan and Kelten-Iva to secure the ship's bridge. Devon-Chi remained standing in the back with Cougar and Tina.

"After we give you a tour of Garden, you're welcome to return to the ship," said Devon-Chi. She had previously explained to the them that most of the ship's crew lived aboard the vessel during visits like this one, a rather fleeting visit of less than an Earth-week for the restocking of supplies and required hull inspections.

"It's a short stay," she said. "But some of the crew will be visiting relatives. My parents live a few kilometers from here. Tina, would you come home with me?"

Cougar thought it was a funny way for her to ask – not just because she was taking Tina home to meet her parents. There was more behind the scenes than struck the eye, and it was obvious in Devon-Chi's voice.

"Sure," replied Tina. "I'd like that."

"Oh, Cougar, I apologize," said Devon-Chi. "I just assumed you wanted to explore on your own and stay with the ship."

"No problem," said Cougar. "You girls just run along now, and I'll be fine. I'd planned to stay on the ship anyway."

When Cougar looked over at Devon-Chi, she was definitely blushing. She quickly turned to Tina, who was brushing away her embarrassment with an obvious gritting of her teeth behind her pouty lips, which were tinted lavender today.

"I hate it when she calls me a girl," said Tina.

\* \* \* \* \*

WHEN THEY STEPPED OUT of the spaceship, it was with a sigh of relief when Cougar took her first breadth of Garden air. They had been thoroughly briefed on what to expect, but it was a tremendous reassurance when her lungs filled with fresh air that felt just like Earth's.

As they exited the ship, military officials greeted them warmly. *Gardenpeace's* crew went first, bowing proudly, and then clasping the upper hands of the officials, while their lower arms swung around each other in human-like hugs. The military representatives were similarly respectful of the humans, although none of them tried to shake their hands or hug them. Instead, they nodded with a slight bow and sincere-looking smiles. For most of these officials, thought Cougar, this was the first time they'd ever seen a live human. Yet there was no intrusion into their personal space.

*Challenger's* crew was now in a group as arranged by Yeleng-Kan, all six of them together in the same small area for the first time since shortly after their second cryogenic sleep session. Together they were led to a nearby hover-transport that looked like a small bus but rested silently a meter off the ground. They stepped up into the vehicle, and as soon as they were seated, the driver-less bus began to move. Yeleng-Kan and one of the military officials remained with them during the ride, the official smiling and nodding to them continuously.

When they stepped inside the building located on the edge of the spaceport, the humans smelled foods they had not encountered on *Gardenpeace*, along with some Earth smells that surprised them.

"Cheese and meatballs!" said Cougar.

"Or maybe lasagna," said Tina. "It looks like they've really done their homework."

"Maybe they're Italians," said Cougar. "It's a lot better than big black pots with boiling water to cook us in."

"Knock it off, Coug," said Tina curtly. "Who knows who speaks what around here. We don't need you mouthing off, or we might find ourselves in one of those pots you imagine."

Then she laughed, to make sure Cougar know she wasn't serious.

The food was delicious, and they ate more than they should have. After nearly an hour of eating and relaxing at their tables (with actual waiters to serve them), the six humans waited to see what would happen next. They had been told they would be offered transport and a planetary host to assist them, but they didn't know exactly what to expect.

Five military women marched into the room in formation, and then halted abruptly near their table. All of them had long flowing hair of bright colors, unlike Devon-Chi's, and all of them were pretty in their own way. By now, the aliens didn't look so strange to the humans. Except for their extra arms, which the humans had slowly gotten used to, they were more normal than expected, considering hundreds of years of science fiction movies on Earth.

The women were young, with smiles reminding Cougar of sports dance teams on Earth – never a crack in their smiles, and never a doubt their grins were somewhat artificial. But it was a class act that was appreciated. Obviously, the alien officials wanted the humans to enjoy their stay on Garden.

The humans didn't know what the protocol was here, but Tina stood up, and the rest of her crew immediately followed suit, moving behind their chairs.

Each of the young women then walked casually to the table, splitting up to go to their assigned humans. They were quick and confident, and they greeted their guests in flawless English.

"Hi, Tim Halmer. I'm Bordaria-Tai. Welcome to Garden."

"Hello, Cougar Jensen. I'm your guide, Ventrella-Dai."

Cougar's assigned hostess had flowing reddish-brown wavy hair, and a pleasant face. It was amazing how quickly you acclimated to a completely different species when there was no language barrier.

"Glad to meet you, Ventrella-Dai," replied Cougar.

"Please call me Dai," said the alien woman.

"And I'm Coug?"

"I hear you're Canadian, eh?"

It was the grandest laugh Cougar had experienced in years. They sure had done their homework. Dai looked back with what seemed a genuine smile.

But then Cougar noticed that no woman had approached Tina, who stood next to her. Just as she began to wonder why, she saw Devon-Chi walking across the room to take her position next to Tina. Her hair was still short, of course, but she'd changed her clothes to a sensual-looking tunic draped over a silky scarlet skirt.

"Hi, you can call me Chi. I'm pleased to be your guide."

*****

Cougar's tour of Garden was well choreographed, with individuals lined along the paths as she walked with Dai to the various places the officials had arranged for her to visit. The beings along the walkways were respectful, always nodding their heads and a quick bow of their body above their lower arms. They were all smiling, and it didn't look artificial. After Cougar and Dai passed, there were murmurs behind them, soft exchanges in the aliens' own tones.

Most of the places they visited were gardens, although some seemed to be designated as memorials. Dai read the words on the signs for Cougar: "In recognition of the crew of Garden spaceship *Dena Trine*, for their contributions to our quest for knowledge," read one inscription, and there were several other gardens dedicated to the planet's spacefaring crews.

"This has been wonderful," said Cougar. "But I'm worn out. Could we go back to the ship?"

"Of course, Coug," said Dai. "Has all of this attention made you uncomfortable? Our people are here to pay their respects to you, you know."

"Oh, no, that's not a problem, although I'm certainly not used to it. The approach and landing took a lot out of me. I guess I really didn't know what to expect, and now seeing all of these... people... is enough to wear me out."

"Sure," said Dai with her proverbial smile. "Let's go back to the ship. It's been a big day, eh?"

Cougar laughed: "Yes, it's been a very big day."

## Chapter 24

## Home

HOME IS WHERE THE HEART IS. It can be on a remote island in the northern lakes of the North American Union, or on a spot of desert in Afro-Europe. Where you eventually find your place in life is home. For the crew of *Challenger*, Garden was now home. For all of their remaining years on the planet, they would never again be tempted to call it Poseidon. Nor would they try to communicate with their original home – the planet called Earth, over a hundred light-years away.

Most of them adapted well to Garden. Kenny Childers and Tim Halmer remained in the planet's space force, engaging in missions to destinations farther away than they had ever dreamed. Kenny became a trusted steward on a gigantic ship called *Butterwild*, and Tim kept his officer rank on a smaller vessel that traveled to the colonies of Earth that had been previously visited by ships like *Gardenpeace*. He provided health services to the colonists, and dispensed drugs freely, as he always had done for his own crew. Kenny and Tim seldom returned to Garden at the same time, but they shared a small home on the shore of one of the planet's many lakes. Much of Garden's population spent their lives near the water.

The lakes were places where independence was cherished, partly because individuals had the freedom to operate personal watercraft. Garden's hover-routes were so advanced and crowded that only automated vehicles were allowed. With the growth of the planet came sacrifices, one of them being overcrowding of the skies and hoverways. Individuals never flew by themselves, nor did they drive a personal hovercraft any more. But on the lakes, you could still pilot your own vessel. Inhabitants of the lakeside homes liked to visit their neighbors in their own watercraft. They enjoyed stopping for groceries at a marina dock, or just hopping aboard and going for a ride on the placid waters. Whether Tim and Kenny were together or apart, they traveled extensively on the lake, meeting comfortably with other residents, and enjoying evenings in the garden-filled marinas. Sometimes they conversed as best they could in the native language of soft murmurs and wavering tones, and they always managed to be understood. And sometimes their dear alien friends took the time to learn English, often floundering as they spoke, but the two humans who loved these people so much always appreciated it.

Tina and Devon-Chi became an inseparable pair. Cougar spent a lot of time with them in the new home Tina and Chi had fabricated for themselves on a lake near the spaceport. The three women would bound around in a watercraft, running in circles to jump their own wake. Cougar would go out past the walk-through windshield into the open bow, lie on her stomach, and drape her arms over the side of the vessel as Chi swept them past the mountains that ran right down to the edge of the water. Cougar raised her face to the open wind, remembering her days of navigating in the bow of *Challenger*. Tina would usually sit in the front seat next to Chi, relinquishing her captain's authority to a companion she loved so dearly.

Cougar couldn't seem to settle down like the rest. She spent some time in space, learning the duties of the bow position of the big ships, similar to the navigator she had once been. The alien ships even utilized the equivalent of donuts for position fixes and noodles for maneuvering. But generally, she felt unfulfilled, looking for more. While she served on the big ships that followed mining routes to nearby planets and asteroids, she was given full responsibility for navigation. Some of these vessels were older, so she could still employ her skills for a good purpose. But at home on Garden, she felt like a fish out of water. She liked the company of the aliens, but craved the companionships she had known with humans. She missed bunking with Tina, and yearned for more human contact. Yet she could never go back to Earth.

Tina took up the life of a professional spacer. She would never command a vessel again because of her limitations in abilities compared to the aliens, but she remained a high-ranking officer with significant responsibilities on the largest spacecraft that continued to explore new planets. Usually, she served on the same ship with Chi, a luxury offered to those officers brilliant enough to be on the military's A-List, and with special consideration for those who shared their lives with each other.

Kim Lin was happy from the moment he was released from cryo-sleep. Aboard *Gardenpeace*, he roamed the compartments, learning everything he could about the ships amazing systems, appreciating technology more advanced than he ever hoped to discover. And he admired the aliens, for their knowledge was incredible, particularly through the eyes of person like Kim who had dedicated his life to the application of scientific knowledge. He even became a people-person for the first time. While he never seemed to have any close friends back on Earth or aboard *Challenger*, he eagerly engaged with creatures from another world. Kim returned to space as a steward, well below his previous rank as a major in the North American Space Force, but he cherished every minute of it. On long missions into galactic space, he could be found working alongside other stewards to troubleshoot an elusive computer problem or to perform preventative maintenance on subsystems he had to study long hours to understand. He found alien spaceships to be his home.

Doctor Mercedes was a different story. He was graciously accepted into Garden's society, retaining his rank as a doctor in a civilization that put medical personnel at the top of the social pyramid, even above the status of spacefarers. He was repeatedly welcomed, pampered, and honored at public events. His additional credentials as a rare human on the planet provided even more notoriety. But he couldn't adapt to any of it.

Donald Mercedes felt he'd let his own world down, and he'd definitely let himself down. He'd never been much for interpersonal communication, and the situation on Garden made it worse. He refused to learn the native language of wavering tones and body language, and ignored those around him who graciously took the time to learn English. To Doctor Mercedes, the aliens were mere creatures, and he didn't know how to cope with them. So he didn't. Three weeks after the arrival of *Gardenpeace* with the six humans aboard, Dr. Donald Mercedes committed suicide by overdose with a simple pill he had carried all the way from Earth. The local health center had never heard of the drug, and didn't know how to properly treat a human, so Doctor Mercedes died 18 hours after overdosing on a 50-count bottle of aspirin.

* * * * *

"What a memorable day," said Tina.

"Memorable in a lot of ways," replied Cougar. "For one thing the three of us are back in space again, together on the same ship for the first time since we arrived on Garden."

"And if you're looking for another way this is memorable, there's the mission," said Chi.

"True enough," said Cougar. "Two humans and a whatever-you-are headed for one of Earth's colonies. How ironic, eh?"

"Coug, I really don't appreciate it when you call Chi a whatever-you-are," said Tina, half-serious, not wanting things to get out of hand.

"No problem, Coug," said Chi with what looked like a sincere smile. "You're just jealous because you used to bunk with your girlfriend, and now you don't."

"You're right – now I don't," said Cougar. "But if I don't bunk with her, I'm glad you do. Honest."

"Oh, I believe you, girl," said Tina. "You'd never kid around about something like that."

"Survival of the fittest," replied Cougar. "Darwin said it's how we evolve, so I figure you two will parent a little whatever-it-is – something looking like a baby kitten."

"Coug! Stop it!" said Tina.

"Don't you just love it, Chi, when she gets mad like that and pushes out those pouty little lips?" countered Cougar.

They all laughed, until Tina finally calmed down enough to try to find a another subject.

"This is a different kind of ship for you, Coug. How's the bow?"

"Tragically boring," replied Cougar. "Big ships like this really don't need a navigator, but they're the only way to get to the colonies. I notice you two seem pretty busy."

"Not really," said Chi. "We're on the bridge during different shifts, and this is one of the shorter trips for us. No big space jumps, and fully automated maneuvers most of the time."

As they sat at their table in the dining area, a microbot rushed by, bumping against Chi's chair as it swept particles off the floor.

"Oh!" yelled Chi. "Crazy little thing."

"Maybe you should shift to the bigger ships, Coug," said Tina. "It might make you feel better about things, if you had more contact with our colonies. Most of the time, we make a stop at one of the colonial rocks somewhere during a mission."

"I don't feel bad about things, Tina."

"Well, I know you do, at least about lack of human contact. That's nothing to be ashamed of."

"If I could do it all over, I'd do it exactly the same," said Cougar. "I've never regretted going on our mission, and it worked out good in the end."

"Tell that to Mercedes," replied Tina, then tipping her head down as if she regretted saying it.

"Asshole!" said Cougar.

"Well, at least she never holds a grudge," said Tina, as she raised her eyebrows at Chi.

"She's right," said Chi. "There's no need to forgive him now."

"Especially when he's comfortable in a Garden burial mound," added Cougar.

"I never regretted the mission either," said Tina. "We always knew it might be a one-way trip, and it would have probably ended that way even if the ATM hadn't failed."

"One-way, just like all of our colonies," said Cougar. "I still think it's amazing that the only two sources of intelligent life – maybe in the entire galaxy – have been roaming around the same small section of space all this time."

"In most cases, some planets have developed dual colonies," said Chi. "The one we're headed to now was visited by our ships a thousand years ago, before it was colonized by Earth, and now it hosts a colony from both planets."

"Of course, the reason you didn't colonize it a thousand years ago was because you were waiting for Earth to arrive," said Tina.

"Sure, but it wasn't as devious as it sounds," replied Chi. "We knew you were advanced enough to visit a few planets in the local area before you finally realized intelligent life isn't everywhere. We wanted to make sure you selected some prime spots and settled in before we came along. For millions of years we've been watching Earth and waiting. Now we figure it's safe to go back to your colonial planets and work cooperatively, without Earth knowing we exist. Helps our economy a lot, too."

"It figures," said Cougar. "It usually all boils down to money."

They laughed again. But Chi wasn't sure they really understood, so she continued.

"Since we've both been competing for the same rocks in space, it shouldn't surprise you that we're together on some of your colonial planets these days. Our scientists are convinced we developed from the same original seeds, which explains a lot of things. And it seems to make it easier for our two species to get along. Maybe we'll become one someday, at least in my dreams."

"But not in our lifetimes," noted Cougar.

"Which is exactly why each of us has to decide things for ourselves," added Tina. "I want you to know I really believe it, Coug."

"That helps, Tina. That helps a lot."

\* \* \* \* \*

"Final pre-landing thrust adjustment complete," said the Princess-like voice over their English translation headsets. "Pre-landing checklist is complete."

The three women stood next to each other, watching the big screen's live broadcast from the bow. Tina had been scheduled to be on the bridge for landing, but had elected to give away her spot to another officer in order to be with Chi and Cougar.

Chi stood in the middle, one of her lower arms around Tina and the other around Cougar.

"Touchdown in less than three minutes," said Chi, a little louder than necessary, to make sure she was heard over the headsets that were still tight to Tina and Cougar's ears.

The bow camera was looking down on Planet 451, a watery world with a big island nearly centered in the screen. It was the only land visible in this close-up view, although two other large islands – call them mini-continents – were poised on this side of the planet, several more on the other side. Planet 451, home to colonies of both Earth and Garden, was more water than land, with the biggest island over 700 kilometers in breadth. The landing rectangle that appeared directly below them was on an island claimed by colonists from Earth.

"You know what I'm gonna' do, don't you?" said Cougar, pulling one side of her headset down off her ear, while Tina did the same.

"It's pretty obvious," said Tina. "Whatever blows up your skirt, girlfriend."

"I don't own a skirt anymore," replied Cougar.

"Then do it for yourself, and you'll be doing it for me, too," said Tina.

Cougar felt Chi pull her closer with her lower alien arm, a gentle tug accompanied by a soft wavering tone that said: "And for me, too."

Chi released her grip on Cougar, but swung her arm in a wide circle that caused Cougar to stumble forward, and then the alien's lower hand gave her a little push towards Tina. Chi let go of both of them, and stepped back as Tina opened her arms to Cougar. They hung on tight until Princess said: "Touchdown. All systems to shutdown mode."

Cougar released her tight hold on Tina, and pushed herself backwards with extended arms, looking at her friend from a comfortable distance. Then she reached up and took off her headset, handing it to Tina: "I won't be needing this any more."

"I know."

"You're still pouting," Cougar said. "Oh, in case you're wondering – I'll be getting off here."

"Sure," said Tina, tears streaming down her face, on top of a broad smile. "It looks like a good place."

And no one doubted that was exactly as it would be.

"Come visit," said Cougar, eyes intense on Tina.

"Sure. I'll do that, Coug."

"And bring your girlfriend, too," replied Cougar, smiling at both of them, without a hint of regret.

"Find us a watercraft," said Tina. "We'll go for a ride."

"I'll find one for us," promised Cougar. "But you know the rules – I get the bow."

Cougar was finally home.

◊ ◊ ◊ ◊ ◊ ◊

# About the Author

From 1980 to 2005, Wayne Lutz was Chairman of the Aeronautics Department at Mount San Antonio College in Los Angeles. He also served 20 years as a U.S. Air Force C-130 aircraft maintenance officer. His educational background includes a B.S. degree in physics from the University of Buffalo and an M.S. in systems management from the University of Southern California. The author is a flight instructor with 7000 hours of flying experience.

For the past three decades, he has spent summers in Canada, exploring remote regions in his Piper Arrow, camping next to his airplane. The author resides in a floating cabin on Canada's Powell Lake in all seasons, and occasionally in a city-folk condo in Bellingham, Washington. His writing genres include regional Canadian publications and science fiction.

## Nonfiction Titles by Wayne J. Lutz

*Coastal British Columbia Stories*

Up the Lake
Up the Main
Up the Winter Trail
Up the Strait
Up the Airway
Farther Up the Lake
Farther Up the Main
Farther Up the Strait
Cabin Number 5
Off the Grid
Up the Inlet

Coastal BC Living Blog
**PowellRiverBooks.blogspot.com**

## Science Fiction Titles
## by Wayne J. Lutz

*Echo of a Distant Planet*
*Inbound to Earth*
*When Galaxies Collide*
*Anomaly at Fortune Lake*
*Across the Galactic Sea*

Order at:
**www.PowellRiverBooks.com**

www.ingramcontent.com/pod-product-compliance
Lightning Source LLC
Chambersburg PA
CBHW071733080526
44588CB00013B/2010